CHERISHING THE EARTH

CHERISHING THE EARTH

How to care for God's creation

Martin J. Hodson and Margot R. Hodson

MONARCH
BOOKS

Oxford, UK, and Grand Rapids, Michigan, USA

First published in the UK in 2008 by Monarch Books
(a publishing imprint of Lion Hudson plc),
Wilkinson House, Jordan Hill Road, Oxford OX2 8DR.
Tel: +44 (0)1865 302750 Fax: +44 (0)1865 302757
Email: monarch@lionhudson.com
www.lionhudson.com

ISBN: 978-1-85424-841-1 (UK)
ISBN: 978-0-8254-6275-7 (USA)

Distributed by:
UK: Marston Book Services Ltd, PO Box 269, Abingdon, Oxon OX14 4YN;
USA: Kregel Publications, PO Box 2607, Grand Rapids, Michigan 49501

DEDICATION

Dave Steel (1951-2006)

We would like to dedicate this book to the memory of our
dear friend Dave Steel, one of the founders of Sage,
Oxford's Christian environmental group. Dave was a
trained botanist, and a brilliant field naturalist – take a
walk with him, and you had a walking encyclopaedia of
birds, flowers, and insects, not to mention local history.

I (Martin) first met Dave in 1990, when we were both
attending St Aldate's church in Oxford. Dave had the idea
to bring together his passion for the natural world with his
Christian faith. At the time this was considered a pretty
radical thing to do – Christians just did not get involved in
environmental issues. But Dave and his wife Caroline
wanted to form a group to do just that, and Sage was born,
originally St Aldate's Group for the Environment. The
group flourished under Dave's skilful leadership. In time
Sage spilled out from St Aldate's to many churches all over
the Oxford region, and we steadily built a network of
Christians who were concerned for the environment – we
now have several hundred people. Dave was always there,

often taking a very unassuming role. Only three days before he was taken into hospital with his final illness, Dave was in our conservation work party at Boundary Brook Nature Reserve.

Things have changed very greatly since those early days back in 1990. Now it is quite common for archbishops, bishops and other church luminaries to make speeches about the environment, but Dave was well ahead of them all. Dave was a visionary, an inspiration, and a very humble man. His influence was far-reaching. We all loved him and miss him very greatly.

This book would almost certainly never have been written if Dave had not had the vision for Sage, and the vision for linking the environment and faith. We caught that vision, and hope you will too.

Contents

Acknowledgements

We are very grateful to Tony Collins, Simon Cox and Roger Chouler at Monarch for making this book possible, and for the incredible speed at which they moved forward to publication.

This book would not have been the same without the short stories our friends and colleagues provided for us: Jamie Carr, Simon Collings, Ruth Conway, Revd Canon Glyn Evans, Dr Andy Gosler, Seb Mankelow, John Neal, Rt Revd Hilkiah Omindo, James Pender, Dr Mike Pepler, Dr Averil Stedeford, and Adam Twine.

Some wonderful photographs were also provided by friends: Simon Collings, Dr Jeremy Biggs, Dr Andy Gosler, Dr Naoki Kaneyasu, Seb Mankelow, James Pender, Peter Rice, Dr Averil Stedeford, and Karl Wallendszus.

The following people offered us advice and help with various aspects of the book, and we are thankful to them: Prof Tasuku Akagi, Judith Allinson, Robert Aquilina, Dr Jeremy Biggs, Nick Collinson, Revd Canon Christopher Hall, Dr Elizabeth Perry, Revd Dr Mike Perry, and Revd John Robertson.

Thanks to Sir John Houghton for his generous foreword, Prof Cal DeWitt, Dr Krish Kandiah and Rt Revd Colin Fletcher for their commendations.

Throughout the writing of the book we have been supported by the members of Sage, Oxford's Christian Environmental Group – you know who you are!

Cherishing the Earth website

Cherishing the Earth has a supporting website, which gives further information to explore alongside the book. Here you will find:

- Study questions for individuals and church home groups
- Weblinks
- More photographs
- Practical tips for more environmental living
- Updates on some of the fast moving areas

This is hosted on the Hodsons' domain. We hope that you will find it useful.

www.hodsons.org/cherishingtheearth

Foreword

Climate change is now generally recognized as perhaps the biggest and most challenging issue facing our planet. I am writing this on the day after the Committee of the Nobel Peace Prize announced their 2007 award jointly to Al Gore and the Intergovernmental Panel on Climate Change (IPCC) for their work in raising awareness of the issue and its implications for the future of our world. The Fourth Science Assessment Report of the IPCC was published in February 2007 and spelt out even more strongly than before that climate change due to human activities is really happening and will have dire consequences for the environment and especially for the world's poorest people.

To mark the publication of this latest IPCC Report, BBC Radio 4 arranged for their Sunday morning worship service on 11 February 2007 to come from Jesus College, Oxford where Margot Hodson is Chaplain. It was a privilege and pleasure to join with her in organizing the service in which many students took part – the occasion is mentioned at the end of Chapter 10 in their book. In it we worshipped God for the wonder of creation, talked about our scientific understanding of climate change, repented for the devastation that we humans are causing within many parts of creation and committed ourselves to prayer and the challenging action necessary to prevent further damage beyond that to which we are already committed. What was particularly moving about the occasion was the bringing together within an overall atmosphere of worship the wonder, the science, the theology and the practical action.

Our modern lives tend to be so compartmentalized –

science, technology, religion, economics, environment and ethics all treated and thought about separately. What Margot the theologian and Martin the scientist have done in this book is to weave together many different aspects of the contemporary environmental crisis. They explain in a readable and inspiring way, how this integration has been realized in the context of their own personal journey of learning and faith. Their journey began some years ago with a strong conviction of environmental concern but increasingly they have become aware of the enormity of the problems that we now face – problems that demand the application of spiritual as well as material resources for their solution. They finish the book, as we did the Jesus College service, with a strong message of hope. I urge you to join them in this journey as you read their book.

John Houghton
President, John Ray Initiative
13 October 2007

1

A living planet made for God's glory

Suddenly, from behind the rim of the Moon, in long, slow-motion moments of immense majesty, there emerges a sparkling blue and white jewel, a light, delicate sky-blue sphere laced with slowly swirling veils of white, rising gradually like a small pearl in a thick sea of black mystery. It takes more than a moment to fully realize this is Earth . . . home.

Edgar Mitchell, Apollo 14 astronaut, 1971

Introduction

What is it about nature that inspires us? What causes us to gasp at a beautiful sunset, a fragile butterfly or the smile of a small child? How do we value nature and how do we balance its value against other values, particularly human needs and economic gain? How do we live with a concern for the natural world, without becoming "other worldly"? In other words, how do we live real lives in our world as we know it, in a way that is sensitive and yet realistic? If we are Christians, does any of this matter anyway? Should our minds and hearts be set on "higher" things?

If we can answer all these questions in this book, we will have succeeded in our aim of explaining the value of this world and how we should relate to it as something that is precious to God, its creator. We intend to be realistic and practical, but above all we wish to bring a Christian message of hope to those concerned with environmental problems today.

Martin and I are beginning this book while staying in a cottage on the west coast of Connemara in Ireland (see photo 1). The scenery here is rugged and beautiful, with coastal inlets and a backdrop of shadowy mountains. Even short walks are full of amazing natural highlights: choughs flying high and playing in the thermals like stunt pilots; a myriad of different butterflies on the rich coastal meadows; and stonechats perching just tantalisingly beyond the range of my camera zoom. Plovers and oystercatchers, terns and cormorants complete the coastal scene (see photo 2). One could think oneself in heaven, and yet this is very real Earth. It is this reality of our Earth as a place made by God and his concern for this beautiful and fascinating world he has created that we wish to explore.

This is a book that we are very excited to be able to write together. Martin, as an environmental biologist, will explain the natural and scientific questions that the subject raises. In simple terms, how do the various parts of the world work? How do they work together? What has gone wrong? And are there possible solutions? My background is in both geography and theology and so I hope to answer some of the spiritual questions that Christians might bring, and look at some of the human problems and challenges that need to be considered alongside the environmental ones. Our intention is to be readable, while still giving a reasonable amount of depth. If you would like to pursue the subject even further, we have put together a supporting website for the book, which contains study questions and extra resources that might be useful for home groups. Details about the *Cherishing the Earth* website can be found at the front of the book on page 10.

Are people more important than nature?

So how do humans relate to other living creatures, the Earth, and even the universe? As Christians, we believe we find the beginnings of the answer to this at the start of the account of the creation of the world in Genesis chapters one and two. These passages are probably best known for disputes over how the universe came to be created and how long it took! We will be looking at this debate, but we want to start by exploring the relationships that were established. For those who believe in a creator God, these will not be affected by views on the way that the Earth was made.

Genesis and ethical starting points

One of our most unforgettable memories came during a holiday by the Sea of Galilee. We were staying at the Church of Scotland Centre in Tiberias and decided to walk to the Galilee lakeside at 5.30am on New Year's Day to watch the sun rise over the lake (see photo 34). As we sat on the beach in the early morning light, we watched pied kingfishers (*Ceryle rudis*)[1] skim the lake for the fish that occasionally bobbed their heads through the sparkling water. The sun began to burst over the Golan and made a bright trail across the lake. With the sounds of the lapping water and flapping of birds, we turned to our Bible reading notes for the day. Amazingly, we found ourselves reading the first chapter of Genesis. No other words in the Bible could have so fitted the moment. We simply sat and marvelled at the beauty around us.

This story summed up for us several significant things about the creation account. Firstly, we were led to wonder at the beauty of the world that God has created and, in doing so, to wonder about God himself. It is clear that Genesis states that as creation unfolded, God saw that it was "good". We believe that each element of the scene we looked at, from the kingfishers to the rising sun, has intrinsic value to God. He made it for its own sake and so we value it as something good that God has made.

Secondly, we felt ourselves to be very much part of the scene, and this is also a strongly biblical concept. We are part of God's creation and not separate from it. We need to breathe and eat like other creatures to survive. We feel the cold and respond to light. For people whose concern for the environment is so great that it outweighs all other concerns, this may be where their ecological principles are entirely based. This group of people believe humans to be no different from the rest of the living world and propose that, in managing the environment, humans should be treated the same way as all other parts of it. These people will divide into two main ethical groups. Some will be *eco-centric*, considering that the balance of the ecosystem as a whole should be the primary concern, and that can be worked out at a local or even a global level. This group might be particularly interested in the Gaia hypothesis that we will discuss in Chapter 5. Others are *biocentric*, considering that the preservation of each species and even each organism should be considered on an equal basis, including humans. This would be the ethic underlying the concept of animal rights.

With both these groups of views there are those who hold them in a moderate form and those who take them to their logical conclusions. If humans are genuinely no different from the rest of creation, these views could be justifiable even in their strongest form. If we turn again to our account of Genesis, however, we find a different value placed on human life. Genesis 1:26-31 gives a unique role and value to human beings. Most particularly, Genesis states that God made humans "in his own image" (Genesis 1:26). Because of this we find that, though humans are part of creation, they are treated differently in the creation stories.

It is possible to focus on this aspect of the creation account alone. Those who do so can place humans so far above the rest of creation that any action is justified, providing humans will profit from it. This approach is known as *anthropocentric*, and is one that has, at different times and places, been adopted by Christians along with others. Sometimes it has been for the benefit of all humans, but sometimes only for a few stronger people who are in control. The problem with this approach is that it places so much power in the hands of humans that other parts of nature have no protection from our actions.[2]

As we sat on the beach that New Year's morning and reflected on God, his beautiful creation, and the teaching of Genesis 1, we found ourselves instinctively taking a more holistic approach. We realized that we needed to balance the reality of being part of a good creation with value in its own right, with the awareness that we were made in God's image. We had the cognitive perception to reflect on the scene in front of us and, as humans, have the power to influence it for good or ill.

Genesis states that God blessed the fish and the birds after he made them, as well as blessing humans. Within these blessings is an alternative approach, an ethical view that is *theocentric*. This sees God as the ultimate value and, in the light of that, seeks to work out a balance of relationships between the whole of his creation and humans who are made in his image. It creates a situation that Old Testament scholar Chris Wright describes as an "ethical triangle".[3]

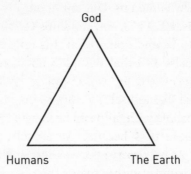

In this diagram, a focus on God and his value for his world begins to make it easier to untangle some of the very difficult environmental problems, where human concerns and environmental needs appear to be in conflict and competition with one another.

We will return to Genesis in the next chapter and will explore our responsibilities within these relationships.

All creation praises God

When we talk about praising God, we usually think of people singing. The setting might be a monastery, with monks chanting beautiful and peaceful psalms, or it might be a large modern church packed with young people, clapping or with hands upraised. Whatever worship style you prefer, the chances are that you will think of people worshipping God. Psalm 148 gives a completely new dimension to our understanding of worship. In this psalm we find that other parts of creation worship God as well as humans. The Sun and Moon, mountains, trees and even lightning and hail are exhorted to worship their maker. How is this possible for non-sentient beings? A tree or a mountain has no brain to understand the concept of God – let alone worship him.

During our walk along the coast of Connemara the beauty of nature overwhelmed us. Our entire universe is made for God's glory (Isaiah 43:7), and worships God by being what it is created to be and doing what it is created to do. It is clear from Psalm 148 that nature is not expected to "do" anything unexpected in worshipping God. When we observe nature "being itself", we are awed, and even those who are not people with faith can be moved to want to give thanks. I believe it is because we are observing nature praising God. As we observe the wonders of creation, so we are caused to wonder at the creator, "his splendour is above the earth and the heavens" (Psalm 148:13). This gives us an understanding of the relationship between God and his non-human creation and helps us to grasp this aspect of the theocentric model outlined above. Having looked at God's concern for the natural world in the Bible, Martin will now explain the wonder of creation in more practical and scientific detail.

Our global ecosystem

It is impossible in this brief account to do more than out-line some of the physical, chemical and biological processes involved in the functioning of the Earth.[4] It is clear, however, that the Earth is incredibly "well designed", and that these processes provided a perfect setting for life to develop.

Expedition up Mount Fuji

"He who climbs Mount Fuji once is a wise man; he who climbs it twice is a fool." (Japanese proverb)

I (Martin) once had the opportunity to accompany two Japanese scientists on a climb to the weather station at the summit of Mount Fuji, the highest mountain (3776 metres) in Japan (see photo 3). The whole visit was a microcosm of environmental science in action. As we walked up the mountain I could ponder the recent volcanic activity that had built this prominent feature of the Japanese landscape. But already I could see hardy plants gaining a foothold – biology had a part to play even in this inhospitable habitat. The effect of the thin air led to one of my colleagues getting altitude sickness, but he recovered at the top. A more humorous event happened when we reached the weather station at the summit. We fancied a cup of tea, but needed to open a new container of milk powder. My friend punctured the paper seal over the container, and milk powder shot out all over the room – another effect of the lowered air pressure.

My other colleague was an atmospheric scientist, who had come to the weather station to set up some special equipment to monitor soot particles in the upper atmosphere. Soot particles are thought to be involved in affecting climate change, but relatively little is known about them. The machine sucked in a volume of air every minute, and then counted the particles on a filter. I reflected on the fact that human pollution could be detected even in this out of the way place. I had plenty of time to reflect on this as we tried to sleep in the same room with the machine sucking its regulation volume of air every minute! The next day we set off back down the mountain in quite windy and wet conditions – the physics of the atmosphere again. At the bottom we were glad to find a hut offering hot cups of bitter green tea. It was not until we returned to Tokyo and I took some plastic water bottles out of my bag that I noticed they had collapsed in on themselves – the effect of the return to sea level. So this was an amazingly intense study of physics, chemistry and biology, all in less than 48 hours.

What did God create?

So what exactly did God create? Of course he made the whole universe, including the Sun, the Moon and the stars (Genesis 1:14-16), but here we are most interested in one small part of the universe: our planet, the Earth. As far as we are aware, the Earth is the only place in the universe that supports life, and, even if life exists elsewhere, it is almost certainly pretty rare. So what is it about the Earth that makes it such a special place, and what are its key features?

It is not possible to discuss these matters without us revealing our thoughts on the age of the Earth. We believe that the evidence points to a very long timescale for the Earth to physically become the way we find it today. We will discuss these issues in more detail in Chapter 5, but are strongly of the opinion that views on the age of the Earth are not that important in deciding whether we should care for it.

The Earth

The Earth is the third in distance from the Sun of the nine major planets in our solar system, and is the fifth largest. The best scientific estimates of the age of the Earth suggest it is about 4.57 billion years old. It is interesting to compare the Earth with its nearest neighbouring planets, Venus the second closest planet to the Sun, and Mars the fourth closest. On Venus the surface temperature is around 400°C, partly because it is closer to the Sun than the Earth, and partly because the planet's atmosphere consists mostly of a thick layer of carbon dioxide, a strong greenhouse gas (see below). On the other hand, Mars has a much thinner atmosphere than the Earth, and the seasonal Martian climate ranges in temperature from -140°C to 20°C. So the Earth is the only one of the three where water can easily be found in all three forms – solid, liquid and gas. Liquid water is essential for life[5], and thus Venus is too hot while Mars is too cold and dry. The Earth is perfect, or at least it is at this time. Early in the planet's history it would have been too cold for life, and millions of years from now, if we are still here to see it, the Earth will be too hot.

Geosphere

If we look at the Earth over geological time, it is seen as a dynamic system with many intricate and complex processes and cycles. The relatively recent science of plate tectonics has shown that the Earth's surface is continually on the move as the plates move apart and rub against each other. Many mountain ranges have been formed as a result. So, for example, the Himalayan Mountains were pushed up as a result of two plates colliding, and they are still rising at a rate of about five millimetres a year. Volcanic activity, such as that at Mount Fuji, also adds to the surface features of the Earth (see photo 4). So does the deposition of sediments, some of which have biological origins and contain fossils. At the same time as these building processes are going on, weathering (physical and chemical breakdown of rock into smaller particles) and erosion (movement of particles from one location to another), wear down rocks. Finally, millions of years after rocks are formed they are eventually sucked back under the plates and are recycled.

Weathering processes are also important in the formation of soil. Most soils are a mixture of small rock particles, organic matter (largely the breakdown products of plant material falling on the soil), water and air. For the vast majority of plants soil is an essential growth medium. The loss of soil through soil erosion is a major environmental problem in many parts of the world.[6]

Hydrosphere

Viewed from space, a better name for our planet might be "Water" rather than "Earth". Of the Earth's surface area 71% is covered by water, and most of that is salt water – the seas. The average depth of the oceans is 4,000 metres, with a maximum of 11,000, but the most biologically productive areas are the continental shelves, which are about 200 metres deep, and surround most of the continents. It is here that most of the fisheries are found, although many are now under threat from overfishing.

In the Bible the sea is a symbol of chaos, and one only has to think of the story of Jonah for an example. The oceans are still to be feared in some respects, and many lives are lost each year because of their unpredictable nature. Few of us will forget the devastating tsunami that hit many countries bordering the Indian Ocean on Boxing Day 2004. This led to about 2–300,000 deaths (estimates vary, and we will almost certainly never know the true number), and much damage to property in coastal areas.[7] Most tsunamis are caused by earthquakes, often through the triggering of landslides in deep crevasses in the ocean floor.

In fact, most of the Earth's water (about 97.3%) is salt water, predominantly in the oceans, but also in salt lakes such as the Dead Sea. Ice caps and glaciers represent about 2.1% of the Earth's water, and these include the basis of whole ecosystems in our Arctic and Antarctic regions. The melting of polar ice and glaciers as a result of global warming is currently a matter of major concern. Only 0.6% of the planet's water is liquid freshwater, mainly as groundwater in aquifers, but with smaller amounts in lakes, rivers and the soil. A comparatively small amount of water (0.001% of the Earth's total) exists at any one time as water vapour in the atmosphere.[8] The world's freshwater supply may represent only a small fraction of the total, but it is vitally important to all terrestrial life including humans. There are considerable concerns as to whether our present use of water in agriculture is sustainable.[9] Droughts from water shortages and floods caused by severe weather events are two of the most serious natural disasters. Water disputes also underlie political tensions in some parts of the world (e.g. the Middle East).

Of course, the water in the hydrosphere is not static, and is continually moving between gaseous, liquid and solid phases in what is known as the hydrological cycle. So water that falls as rain or snow on land may then percolate into underground aquifers or run straight off into lakes and rivers. From there the rivers take the water to the seas. At any stage some of the water is evaporated back into the atmosphere, either directly from the land or water bodies, or indirectly after passing through plants.[10] Within any body of liquid water there are currents, a distinct flow of water from one place to another. The ocean currents move large volumes of water across the Earth's surface. Probably the best-known ocean current is the Gulf Stream, or North Atlantic Conveyor, which brings warm water from the Gulf of Mexico past the east coast of the USA and then across the Atlantic to northern Europe. This gives countries like the UK much milder climates than would otherwise be expected from their latitude.[11] There is a possibility that the melting of the ice caps of Greenland due to global warming could increase cold water flowing into the North Atlantic, and that this would switch off the Conveyor, leading to much lower temperatures along the eastern seaboard of the USA and in northern Europe. This scenario was behind the Hollywood drama *The Day after Tomorrow* (2004)[12], which envisaged an extremely abrupt climate change with a transformation to an Ice Age within weeks. No serious scientists think a change on this timescale is at all likely to happen, and the jury is still out on whether the shutdown of the North Atlantic Conveyor over a longer period is something we need to worry about.

Atmosphere

An intelligent alien looking at our world would immediately recognize that our atmosphere was not that of a dead planet. The air we breathe consists of 78% nitrogen, 21% oxygen and much smaller amounts of a number of other gases. The presence of oxygen, ozone, carbon dioxide and methane all indicate life, and a continually renewed system. The atmosphere gradually thins out above us, as we saw on Mount Fuji, but 90% of air can be found within 20 km of the Earth's surface. Oxygen is, of course, essential for all higher organisms, including us, as it is used in respiration (see below), but this is not the case for many species of bacteria. It is believed that the early atmosphere of the Earth was low in oxygen, and that it was only with the appearance of green plants and the beginning of photosynthesis that oxygen levels increased.

Carbon dioxide and methane are present in our atmosphere in very small quantities, but they are excellent at trapping heat as it is radiated back from the Earth's surface, and without these gases the planet would be too cold to sustain life (about 15°C below present temperatures). The reason carbon dioxide and methane are called "greenhouse gases" is because they let in solar radiation, but decrease the amount of infrared radiation escaping through the atmosphere. As we will see later, human-induced changes in the concentrations of these gases are creating major problems by causing our climate to change.

Ozone in the upper atmosphere filters out most of the ultraviolet radiation from the Sun. This is important for humans, as too much ultraviolet is a cause of skin cancer. It was therefore of some concern when scientists in the 1970s discovered an "ozone hole" over the Antarctic. The major cause of the problem was soon discovered to be chemicals known as freons or CFCs (chlorofluorocarbons), which cause the breakdown of ozone. CFCs have many industrial uses, but most particularly in refrigeration systems.[13] Fortunately the international community took prompt action through the Montreal Protocol in 1987, and CFC production has been steadily cut back. The ozone hole problem is not entirely "solved", but most people think it is at least under control.

Like the oceans, the atmosphere is in a continual state of movement. Winds are important in a number of ways, including the transfer of heat from one part of the planet to another, the transport of moisture and the resulting precipitation, and the movement of pollutants.[14] Strong winds, hurricanes and tornados are the cause of much damage and loss of life every year. One of the predictions with global warming is that the frequency and intensity of such events will increase (see Chapter 3).

Energy and cycles

The energy that drives most of the processes on the Earth, whether physical, chemical or biological, originates from the Sun. Only about 0.1% of the incoming radiation from the Sun is trapped by green plants in photosynthesis, but that is a key process, as the energy is used to convert carbon dioxide in the atmosphere into simple sugars. These simple sugars are the building blocks for more complex carbohydrates, proteins and many other organic (carbon-containing) compounds. Without photosynthesis and plants there would be nothing for animals to eat, and the biblical saying "All flesh is grass..." (Isaiah 40:6, KJV), has much truth. The biochemical process of respiration that is carried out by all animals and plants is, in many respects, the reverse of photosynthesis. Sugars are broken down using oxygen, release carbon dioxide into the atmosphere, and liberate energy to drive complex systems such as muscle movement and brain activity. Of course, sooner or later, all plants and animals die and decompose, and their carbon is mostly released back into the atmosphere. The above is just one example of a biogeochemical cycle, and such cycles exist for all elements, including nitrogen, phosphorus and potassium. The cycling of energy and elements within the Earth system is very elegant, and in some respects resembles a self-regulating system.

Our global ecosystem: Conclusion

So the Earth that God made is a very remarkable place. We have held back from discussing the Earth's organisms, or its biodiversity, as this will be a major strand of the next chapter. Even at this stage, however, it is worth pointing out that there is not one system on Earth that has not been affected by human actions. We have plundered its mineral resources and polluted the land, the atmosphere and the water. There is little doubt that we face an environmental crisis in the 21st century. We therefore urgently need to learn how to care for God's creation, and this will be the focus of our book.

Partners with God for a fruitful planet

You ask what is the use of butterflies? I reply to adorn the
world and delight the eyes of men; to brighten the
countryside like so many golden jewels. To contemplate
their exquisite beauty and variety is to experience the
truest pleasure. To gaze enquiringly at such elegance of
colour and form devised by the ingenuity of nature and
painted by her artist's pencil, is to acknowledge and
adore the imprint of the art of God.

John Ray[1]

Have you ever sat on a park bench and pondered life, the
universe and everything? I would be surprised if you have
ever thought about the actual bench in its previous life as a
living tree, possibly in some other part of the world. It may
have been grown in a plantation and replaced after felling.[2]
It is sadly possible that your bench could have been a wild
tree – maybe a tropical hardwood – that was cleared for a
one-off profit for the contractor. The land exposed might
yield a useful crop for a few short years, but the soil is far
too thin to survive without its protective covering of trees.
So the cost of your bench could be the change from a living
and productive forest to a degraded piece of land or even a
semi-desert. The rate of deforestation worldwide is alarm-
ing – in 2003 deforestation of the Amazon was 40% higher

than it had been in 2001 and 10% of the world's tree species face extinction because of exploitation.[3]

What is our responsibility for the world?

If humans are a part of nature but also created in God's image, it is reasonable to conclude that our role within nature will be different from that of other species. If we go back to the first couple of chapters in Genesis we find this role outlined in two different ways. In the first chapter we are given the following command:

> Be fruitful and multiply, and fill the earth and subdue it; and have dominion over the fish of the sea and over the birds of the air and over every living thing that moves upon the earth (Genesis 1:28, NRSV).

This has been misunderstood to mean that people can do what they like with the rest of creation, and it has even been suggested by some that people should beat nature into submission! The original command meant something very different. The term "dominion" (*radah*) means "to rule over" and is used in the Old Testament to describe the benevolent rule of the good Israelite kings over their subjects. The term "subdue" (*kabash*) is related to working the soil and is a command to interact with nature and aid its fruitfulness.[4] So the verse might be better translated as:

> Be fruitful and multiply; fill the earth and work the soil; and have responsibility for the fish of the sea and for the birds of the air and for every living thing that moves upon the earth.

The responsibility of leadership over the rest of nature comes directly from being made in God's image and we are therefore answerable to God for the quality of our rule over his Earth.

This responsibility is presented in a more pictorial way in Genesis 2. This chapter describes the planting of a garden by God as a home for Adam and Eve. Verse 15 describes God's intentions:

> The LORD God took the man and put him in the garden of Eden to till it and keep it (Genesis 2:15, NRSV).

"Till" is the verb for "work" (*avad*). This word also means "serve". Later, when Israel had priests, they would serve (*avad*) God in the Temple, and so it also means "worship" when used in the context of serving God. Likewise, the word for "keep" (*shamar*) is highly symbolic. The Israelite priests were commanded to "keep" their priest's office by caring for the Lord's altar (Numbers 18:7). In Genesis 28:20, Jacob, after fleeing from his brother, has a dream at Bethel in which God promises to keep (protect) him. In Psalm 37:28 the Lord is said to "keep" the righteous, and, in Numbers 6:24, the Aaronic blessing begins: The Lord bless you and keep you. Cal DeWitt, a leading Christian environmentalist, describes this word as meaning to care and protect something in a way that will give life to it.[5]

We can therefore understand that humans have been given responsibility for the rest of the created world. We are expected to interact with it and adapt it, but we should do so in a way that is for the good of nature as well as ourselves. If we are tilling and keeping properly, the whole of creation will flourish, and we will see the God-given biodiversity of our planet reach its full potential. To help us understand this more fully, Martin will explain what biodiversity means.

Biodiversity

The word "biodiversity" has had a pretty rapid rise to fame. It was coined in 1985 by W.G. Rosen as a shortening of "biological diversity". The word has now spread beyond the scientific community, and a search on Google revealed 27 million hits on web pages in 2007. But what does it mean, and why is it important? Again, we can hope to give only a brief overview of the topic here, and the interested reader is referred to Gaston and Spicer (2004) for more information.[6]

Definition and Numbers

Biodiversity has proven difficult to define, and there are many different definitions. Most simply, Gaston and Spicer say biodiversity is "the variety of life"[7] A more complex definition was provided by the Convention on Biological Diversity, which was signed by 150 world leaders at the Rio Earth Summit in 1992:

> "Biological diversity" means the variability among living organisms from all sources including, *inter alia*, terrestrial, marine and other aquatic ecosystems and the ecological complexes of which they are part; this includes diversity within species, between species and of ecosystems.

Scientists do not know precisely how many species there are in the world, but estimates range from 3 to 30 million, of which about 2.5 million have been classified. These include 900,000 insects, 41,000 vertebrates and 250,000 plants (see Photos 5 and 6). The remainder are invertebrates, fungi, algae and microorganisms. Whatever estimate of the total number of species we take, it is obvious that there are still a large number that we have not recognized. Most of these are relatively small, but even now almost every year we discover some quite large plant or animal that was previously unknown to science.

Distribution

The world's biodiversity is not evenly spread. In the UK certain habitats, such as chalk grasslands, have much higher biodiversity than others such as pine forests. In general, the world's tropical rainforests are much more diverse than any temperate habitat, which in turn have higher diversity than the Arctic or Antarctic. For example, Brazil contains a particularly large number of animal and plant species, and only seventeen countries[8] are thought to contain 75% of the world's biodiversity.[9] There are certain areas, known as biodiversity hotspots, where the number of organisms present is very high indeed. Norman Myers, the Oxford environmental scientist, and his colleagues found that 44% of land plants and 35% of mammals, birds, reptiles and amphibians were concentrated in 25 hotspots, which accounted for only 1.4% of the Earth's surface.[10] Of these 25 hotspots, three appeared, using a variety of criteria, to be the hottest: Madagascar, the Philippines and Sundaland (the Malay Peninsula, Sumatra, Java, Bali, and Borneo). These are areas that conservationists particularly want to protect, but sadly they are under major threat.

Measuring biodiversity in the seas has proven to be more complex than on land. It seems, however, that there are more groups (e.g. phyla) of organisms in the seas, but more individual species on land. It is generally thought that marine biodiversity is highest in the tropical regions, and particularly in the Indo-western Pacific.

The Wollemi Pine

In the summer of 2006, Margot and I visited the National Botanic Gardens at Glasnevin in Dublin.[11] Whenever we are in a city we always track down its gardens, and I guess this is an occupational hazard of being married to a plant scientist. It was a warm, sunny afternoon, and the plants were wonderful, but one, in the part of a greenhouse reserved for tender gymnosperms (a group of seed bearing plants, which include the conifers), really grabbed our attention. It was a rather shaggy looking effort, but one that was obviously special, as it was the only tree behind bars. This was a Wollemi Pine (*Wollemia nobilis*), and it had been planted by the Taoiseach, Mr Bertie Ahern, only the previous September. You may well ask why this plant was so well protected, and why the Irish Prime Minister took time out to plant it. The answer is that the Wollemi Pine is a "living fossil" because it was thought to be extinct before September 1994. It was then that David Noble, a wildlife officer in New South Wales, Australia, ventured into a remote canyon in Wollemi National Park, and found a plant that had until then been known only from the fossil record. The population of Wollemi Pines in the wild is less than a hundred mature trees, and an international effort is now under way to conserve this rare species.[12] The tree planted by Mr Ahern was the first to be planted on Irish soil, and is part of the conservation schemes to preserve this plant. The story of the Wollemi Pine well illustrates that there are still even quite large species of plants and animals that have yet to be discovered, and it is almost certain that some species have become extinct without our even knowing.

Benefits of biodiversity

Why is biodiversity important? When present estimates suggest that there are millions of species on Earth, does it really matter if we lose a few, or even a considerable number? The answer to this question will depend to a large extent on which of the ethical views, outlined in Chapter 1, that you take. An often-cited reason for protecting biodiversity is that there might be some unknown species out there that could be useful to humans. Somewhere in the Amazon basin there may be a plant that contains an important anti-cancer or anti-AIDS drug. At present we use very few plant species as agricultural crops, and rely very heavily on only three: wheat, maize and rice. There may be new potential crops among the many species that have not been described. It is also possible that there are related species of our present crop plants, which could be used to introduce disease resistance characteristics into a crop. There may be insects that could be used in biological pest control. All these valuable resources may be being lost. This is all true, and it is a good reason for protecting biodiversity, but of course it is a very anthropocentric reason.

Another idea says we need to maintain the integrity of the Earth's systems, so that life on Earth can flourish. There is a concern that if we lose too much biodiversity then too many links in the system will be broken. The removal of one or a few species may, or may not, cause damage to an ecosystem, but obviously the more that are removed the more "connections" are broken, and the more likely it is that the whole system will become unstable and collapse. Protecting biodiversity to save ecosystems can be ecocentric, but if we are doing this to ensure human survival, then it can also be tinged with anthropocentrism. We can also find ourselves in the situation of protecting biodiversity and habitats in order to increase the numbers of some species or group of species that we consider to be particularly desirable. For instance, many nature reserves are set up with the specific purpose of providing suitable habitats for birds, and others are protected for just one species (e.g. the Wollemi Pine). In some circumstances, this reasoning could verge on biocentric.

All the views above will result in the protection of some biodiversity, but they all tend to leave some species out because they are not "useful" or "pretty", large enough to be easily visible, or whatever. Only when we protect biodiversity holistically for its intrinsic value will we maximize protection, and decrease the loss of species.[13]

Biodiversity in the Bible

The biblical writers appreciated a rich biodiversity. We know this because the pages of the Bible are buzzing with insects, alive to the song of birds, majestic in their description of trees and awesome in appreciation of the strength of large animals. The Bible contains the names of countless species of trees and animals. There are thirteen different Hebrew words for owls alone and nine for locusts.[14] Knowledge of natural history was greatly prized. When the wisdom of Solomon was described in 1 Kings 4:33, it was expressed in terms of his being able to describe plant life, animals, birds, reptiles and fish.

Some species had symbolic meaning in connection with the Land of Canaan. In Deuteronomy 8:8, seven species are mentioned as fruits of the land: barley, wheat, vines, figs, pomegranates, olives and dates (honey). Each year, the first of these fruits to be gathered were offered at the Temple in thanks to God for the annual harvest. The reason for this was to ensure that the Israelites did not forget the Lord, when they finally gained land to farm. They were instead encouraged to rejoice for the abundance of the harvest. During the autumn harvest feast of Tabernacles, the Israelites were commanded to take choice fruit with branches of palm, willow and myrtle and "rejoice before the Lord" (Leviticus 23:40). This tradition still continues with the beautifully fragrant citrus fruit, the etrog, and the branches bound together and waved in synagogues and at the Western Wall in Jerusalem.[15]

Animals are a particular feature of the book of Isaiah, where they are mentioned at least 160 times.[16] There is considerable interest in their behaviour, which is usually seen positively. Some are domestic, such as the ox and the ass in Isaiah 1:3, who are described as more obedient than God's people. Others are wild, but they are rarely portrayed negatively and are even named as those who honour God because they know he provides for them (Isaiah 43:20). The most famous animal passage in Isaiah is 11:6–9, describing the wolf lying down with the lamb. In terms of biodiversity this implies that there is a place for all creatures in God's future kingdom.[17]

Habitats

Having considered the organisms from the perspective of biodiversity, we must now move on to consider the places where plants and animals live. The place where a particular species lives and grows is often called a habitat. An ecosystem includes all the organisms in an area, and the abiotic (non-living) factors they interact with. On a larger scale, a biome is the flora and fauna that live in a habitat and occupy a certain type of geography. Before we sketch the major biomes of the world, let us start with an investigation conducted on a much smaller scale.

Temporary ponds

In the spring and early summer of 1992 one of my undergraduate project students, Nick Collinson[18], was carrying out the fieldwork for his project. Nick was co-supervised by Jeremy Biggs of Pond Action[19], and we had set him the task of surveying the temporary ponds (those ponds that routinely dry up) in the Oxford area for aquatic macroinvertebrates.[20] Conventional wisdom had it that temporary ponds were not very important habitats for biodiversity, and certainly not as good as permanent ponds (see photo 7). It soon became evident that things were not as simple as that. In one very unpromising looking temporary pond near Fringford, north of Oxford, Nick found *Haliplus furca-tus*, a Red Data Book 1 (endangered) species of water bee-tle. *H. furcatus* had previously been recorded in the UK only in North Somerset in 1916, South Somerset in 1935–7, and West Norfolk in 1987, and so it was truly a rare beetle![21]

Overall, Nick's data showed that the temporary ponds had quite a number of rare species in them. They did not have as many species as permanent ponds, but they had different species, and were valuable habitats for biodiver-sity. Nick's work was so interesting that we combined it with some other data from Pond Action and wrote it up as a paper.[22] The paper helped to convince scientists and con-servationists around the world of the importance of tem-porary ponds for biodiversity. It also suggested a number of ideas for the management of these habitats. The key point was that digging a pond out to increase its "perma-nence" could be highly damaging. Temporary ponds are important habitats in their own right for biodiversity, and are just different from permanent ponds, not inferior to them.

Major biomes

There are many different ways of categorizing habitats. We could start by dividing them into terrestrial (on land) and aquatic (in water) biomes. Campbell, Reece and Mitchell divided the terrestrial biomes into nine major types: tropi-cal forest; savannah (a type of grassland with widely spaced trees); desert; polar and high-mountain ice; chaparral (shrub land particularly associated with Mediterranean climates); temperate grassland; temperate deciduous forest; coniferous forest; and tundra (arctic and alpine).[23] Undoubtedly, the major factor in determining which terrestrial biome is present in a particular location is the climate. The aquatic biomes include both freshwater and marine categories. Campbell et al. suggest seven major aquatic biomes: lakes; rivers; estuaries (often of variable salinity); intertidal zones (rocky shores, beaches, etc.), coral reefs; oceanic pelagic (the main part of the oceans); and abyssal zones (very deep parts of the ocean floor).

Habitats familiar to Jesus

Having looked at the different categories of habitat, it is interesting to see which of them occur in the Bible. It is not possible to make a direct comparison between the habitats in the Bible lands today and how they might have been in the biblical period. This is because many have been altered through agriculture, changing climate or war. When Napoleon retreated from the Holy Land, for example, he ordered a scorched earth policy, and today's land can give a false impression of the land that Jesus would have known because it would have been far more forested in the 1st century. Even the trees that we do see today may not be native. The Australian eucalyptus is now quite common, but was introduced in the 19th century to help drain swamps.

We need to take these changes into account when we look at Bible habitats. We can discover this environmental history from field investigation and historical records as well as from environmental archaeology. Once you gain an awareness of this, it is possible to get a very good idea of the environmental world that Jesus would have known from visiting Israel and some of the other Bible lands.

Hill pasture and forest

Hills and valleys surround Jesus' hometown of Nazareth, and this was typical of the areas of Israelite settlement in biblical Canaan. The soil was fairly fertile and the climate was Mediterranean with spring and autumn rains. Farming was mixed, with grazing for animals, vineyards and trees providing fruit, nuts and oil. Fields were ploughed for barley and wheat, and these were harvested from April to late May. The famous passage in Matthew 6:25–34, about the birds of the air and the lilies of the field, draws on images from this habitat. With no herbicides, both the pastures and the grain fields would have been colourful with flowers. Birds would have been common in the fields and possibly not too popular with the farmer! This landscape was the ecological basis of the "land of milk and honey" (Exodus 3:8). The grazing animals produced milk and the flowers of the field provided pollen and nectar for bees.[24] When the Israelites first entered the land, this environment was not as fertile as the coastal plains, but perfect for their pastoral way of life.

Where farming was not practised, these uplands were covered by a Mediterranean shrubland known as "Maquis"[25], and here the main species was the evergreen kermes oak.[26] Other tree species would have included terebinth, hawthorn and wild olive. There are passages in the Old Testament that give evidence of the woodland cover being cleared for agriculture; for example, in Joshua 17:14–18, the tribe of Joseph complain because they don't feel that they have enough land. Joshua tells them to go up into the hill country and clear the forest for land.

Deserts

Deserts feature significantly in the Old Testament and are the place where people went to seek God (see Photo 8). Likewise, Jesus spent 40 days fasting in the desert before starting his ministry. The sort of habitat described can be experienced in places such as Ein Gedi to the west of the Dead Sea. It is an arid area of deep ravines with dry riverbeds and occasional springs. Heavy rain further up will cause flash floods and so care needs to be taken when walking in this dramatic landscape. Though described as desert, it is not totally barren. The Bedouin have lived in this region for centuries by becoming skilled in knowing which of the sparse drought tolerant plants can be eaten or used for their sheep and goats. As a skilled shepherd, King David lived as a fugitive in the area, sheltering in caves and surviving in this arid environment by following a nomadic lifestyle.

Aquatic habitats

Overall, the eastern end of the Mediterranean area has a relatively dry climate with rain mainly in the winter and long dry summers when many streams and lakes dry up. This is why water was so important and is used as a metaphor in many places. Jesus would have known some aquatic habitats. At the start of his ministry, he moved to Capernaum on the shores of the inland Sea of Galilee. This is a beautiful lake, fringed with reeds and rich in fish and bird species. Flowing into and out of the lake is the River Jordan (see Photo 32). This remains through the summer, fed from the rains on Mount Hermon higher up. The upper end is particularly rich in water-loving plants and animals.

Biblical exotics

We last visited upper Galilee in the early spring, staying at Kfar Blum Kibbutz on the shores of the Jordan River, fringed by the inevitable eucalyptus trees. It was a real treat to rise at dawn and walk along the river, spotting wildlife each morning. Our favourite was the native white-breasted kingfisher (*Halcyon smyrnensis*)[27] skimming down the river in the early morning light. It was stunningly beautiful and vibrantly alive, and the first time we saw it we were so taken by surprise that we nearly missed its distinctive brown head and white breast amid the brilliant blue that is similar to the European kingfisher. Kingfishers remind me of the way the Holy Spirit works in our lives.

When we feel his touch, we catch just a glimpse of the full wonder of our God.

On our early morning walks, our biggest surprise was a sighting of the ring-necked parakeet (*Psittacula krameri*).[28] This large and very colourful bird is an exotic species introduced as a pet, and it looked completely out of place in its biblical surroundings. There is now a feral population in Israel that is able to breed successfully and this one was probably living on the fruit and nuts from the surrounding orchards of the kibbutz.

Our last exotic was of a different nature. Further up the Jordan River we came to what looked like a boathouse with a sign in Hebrew. Our translation did not make sense until we vocalized it: "Misada Pagoda HaYardan" – "misada" means restaurant in Hebrew, and "HaYardan" is the Jordan. This was the local oriental restaurant and we later had a beautiful meal, served by the Vietnamese owners, who had come to the country as refugee boat people. As we sat by the banks of the Jordan, we reflected on the internationalization of our world.

When we seek to be stewards of our planet we need to care for a world that has been heavily influenced by humans. We cannot put the clock back but, if we embrace the world as it is, we can see the potential for a future, in which natural and human influenced elements of our "nature" can coexist if we nurture them wisely.

Natural habitats?

In Chapter 4 we will look at some of the very serious impacts humans have had on biodiversity and on habitats. But before we get to that it is worth considering whether there are any habitats left in the world that have not been affected by humans. We saw in the last chapter that it was possible to detect soot particles at the top of Mount Fuji.

As long ago as 1962, Rachel Carson, in her famous book *Silent Spring*, reported that pesticide residues were being found in the tissues of organisms very considerable distances from where the chemicals were originally used.[29] We all carry traces of radioisotopes from past nuclear tests. So it is probably true to say that at a chemical level there are now no environments or organisms that do not show some signs of human impact if we look hard enough.

What about the larger scale? Are any of the landscapes we see around us "natural"? Take for an example, Connemara in the west of Ireland, where we spent an idyllic holiday in 2006 (see Photo 1). The landscape with its mountains, coastal scenery and peat bogs is beautiful, but it is very much influenced by human activity. After the last Ice Age forests began to develop in Connemara, but when people arrived they started to chop the forest down for wood and to provide land for agriculture. The high rainfall in the area fairly rapidly led to the development of peat bogs. So what we see now in Connemara is stunning, but certainly not natural. In fact there are almost no habitats in the United Kingdom and Ireland that are not affected by humans. It is a similar story in most of Europe, with the possible exceptions of some mountain areas and the far north. However, in some parts of the world there are still fairly significant areas of almost untouched wilderness.

Conclusion

The biblical concept of stewardship is one in which humans are partners with God in caring for his world. We are both part of nature and also set apart from it, as creatures made in God's image. Our call is not to keep well away from nature (even if we could!) but to interact with the rest of the natural world. The Bible takes a very positive view of farming and adapting natural ecosystems. This way of life is blessed by God, providing that it is undertaken in a way that is sensitive to the needs of the rest of nature. Our interaction should be bringing life and fruitfulness, rather than draining the Earth of its resources. When we look ahead, we also see a domesticated rather than a wilderness ideal: God promises a future where people will plant vineyards and eat their fruit, build houses and enjoy the work of their own hands (Isaiah 65:21–25). We can conclude that the biblical pattern is one of stewardship, foreseeing the impact of careful "tilling and keeping" of the earth, and not afraid of presenting a fruitful domesticated vision as part of God's future plan for his planet.

It is easy to miss this either by thinking that the ideal is to return to wilderness, without human intervention, or because we dissociate our faith from our actions towards the Earth. Environmentalist Eilon Schwartz teaches that our responsibility is to understand not how we can leave nature untouched, but how we can touch nature.[30] In the 21st century, humans have so much power over all habitats and all other species that we need to develop management plans for our domesticated landscapes and for those areas we perceive as wilderness. If we take a theocentric view, then all the habitats we interact with, from our backyards to a mountain range, should be managed by the fruitfulness principle. We must first take responsibility for good stewardship of the environments in which we live and work. This will better equip us to approach the conservation of more awesome and fragile habitats that are now so under threat.

Pushing the planet into free fall

Global warming is now a weapon of mass destruction. It kills more people than terrorism, yet Blair and Bush do nothing.

Sir John Houghton[1]

Environmental degradation

Some years ago I (Martin) was very fortunate to be able to go to a place that had been on my list for years. Jews and Christians want to go to Jerusalem, and Muslims to Mecca: people interested in metal toxicity in plants all want to go to Sudbury in north Ontario, Canada.[2] Sudbury is about 400 miles north-west of Toronto in a vegetation zone that is transitional between the coniferous forest to the north, and the deciduous forest to the south. Sudbury's problems originated in 1872 when lumbering began, leaving great areas of land exposed to soil erosion. Most of the trees went to help rebuild Chicago after the great fire of 1871.

Some previous work had suggested metal ores were present, but it was in 1885 that a large nickel deposit was located, and a mine opened the following year. The nickel ore was mixed with iron and copper ore. All three ores were found to be high in sulphur, which had to be removed. The method used was to create an open-air roast yard. The ore was first crushed and then piled onto wooden beds and ignited. After one to two months of burning, the ore was taken to a smelter for further processing. There were lots of problems with this, but two of the major ones were sulphur dioxide air pollution, and the cutting down of yet more forests. The smelters, which were not very efficient, added more sulphur dioxide and particles containing copper and nickel to the atmosphere. By 1901 there were 80 roast heaps and nine furnaces in the area.

The pollution was so bad by 1929 that open bed roasting had to be abandoned. The first systematic study of the sulphur dioxide pollution took place in 1944. The pollution was burning the leaves off trees 55 km from the city, could be smelt 60 km away, and could be seen 110 km away. At its peak in 1960, Sudbury alone produced 2.56 million tonnes of sulphur dioxide, a staggering 4% of global emissions at the time. So this complex series of events led to permanently denuded land in Sudbury (see photo 9).

By 1970 there were 20,000 hectares of almost completely barren land in the vicinity of the smelters, 80,000 hectares of semi-barren land further away, and 7,000 acid damaged lakes. The land was so barren that a local legend relates that the Apollo astronauts practised there before the moon landings! Actually, the astronauts used the area's 1.8 billion year old meteorite crater to study lunar impact sites, but it is easy to see how the myth developed. In the most barren areas the plants must deal with a soil that has a very high acidity, largely as a result of previous smelting. High copper and nickel levels in the soil resulted from the fallout of particles, mostly from early inefficient smelting and roast beds. Copper and nickel are far more toxic in acid soils as they are much more available for plant uptake. Aluminium is also very high in these acid soils.

Long after the roast yards had closed, and more

efficient smelters with taller stacks were installed, the soil pollution problems remained, and, copper, nickel and aluminium toxicity caused major difficulties for plant growth. The good news was that a highly successful clean up operation was undertaken, led by scientists from Laurentian University in Sudbury, and the companies running the metal smelters. Between 1970 and 1995, a 90% reduction in sulphur dioxide and metal particulate emissions had been achieved. In recent years, the Sudbury Regional Land Reclamation Program has planted eight million trees. So Sudbury has made great strides forward, and is now beginning to leave its polluted past behind.

The story of Sudbury is a good example of local pollution, in that the metal contamination was largely concentrated in a relatively small area within about 30 km of the city. However, the sulphur dioxide that was and still is produced spreads much further, and is an example of regional pollution. We will come back to this type of regional pollution shortly, but first some biblical insights from Margot.

The land mourns

The prophet Hosea has a very contemporary feel when we read his words in the light of the story of the devastation of Sudbury:

> Hear the word of the Lord, you Israelites, because the Lord has a charge to bring against you who live in the land: "There is no faithfulness, no love, no acknowledgement of God in the land. There is only cursing, lying and murder, stealing and adultery; they break all bounds, and bloodshed follows bloodshed. Because of this the land mourns, and all who live in it waste away; the beasts of the field and the birds of the air and the fish of the sea are dying." (Hosea 4:1–3)

Hosea takes us, dramatically, into a courtroom and brings the sins of God's people before us, as a prosecuting counsel lays out his case in front of witnesses.[3] We too can feel under this charge as we read the catalogue of disasters our species is unleashing on God's Earth. Hosea was speaking to the people of Israel, or the northern tribes, who had become syncretistic in their faith and had not kept covenant with their Lord. God has placed us all under an obligation to be stewards of the Earth and as Christians we are particularly aware of our responsibility from our covenant relationship with him. Has our entire human race reached a point when it has "broken all bounds"? Can this passage be applied to our contemporary situation at all, and what does it mean?

For Hosea's listeners the case was already proved and the passage gives the sentence in graphic terms. The phrase "the land mourns" can also imply "the land dries up": these ideas had become interconnected in Canaan because of the practice of mourning during times of drought.[4] Hosea could not have described a picture of drought more vividly: the people are described as "wasting away", the crops have failed and famine is sweeping through the land; the large land animals suffer first, then the birds, and finally even the sea dries up and the fish are left stranded and dying. There is an ambiguity in the tenses of this passage and it is not certain whether it is written in the present, so that Hosea is speaking while these events are happening; or whether it should be in the future, and Hosea is warning that this will be the consequence of disobedience; either way, the judgement is severe.

Though we are aware that Hosea gives a specific judgement for a specific situation, we must also be conscious that God has laid out the consequences for our misuse of the Earth he has given to us. If this is a "snapshot" of what could happen in Hosea's day, what picture have we created? Our natural environments are affected not only by "natural" stresses such as drought, but by major disasters of our own making, which have degraded and polluted our natural world.

Acid rain

Much of the sulphur dioxide produced by smelters such as those at Sudbury reacts with water vapour in the atmosphere to produce sulphuric acid. The burning of coal (which also often has a high sulphur content), and other industrial processes, has a similar effect. When this falls to earth we have the phenomenon of acidic precipitation, popularly called "acid rain". But sulphur dioxide is not the only such problem. The internal combustion engine (principally in our cars) burns nitrogen in the atmosphere with oxygen to produce nitrogen oxides. The nitrogen oxides can in turn react with water vapour, resulting in nitric acid. Since the Industrial Revolution a cocktail of sulphuric and nitric acids has been falling in the rain across much of the developed world. Because of the prevailing winds, much of the acid rain produced in the UK falls in North Europe and Scandinavia. So this type of pollution can spread hundreds of miles, and acid rain is a good example of regional pollution.

In the late 1970s, trees in the forests of Western Europe and North America began to die in large numbers. This was particularly noted in the Black Forest in Germany, and the word the Germans used for the problem, *"Waldsterben"* (literally "forest dying"), was soon adopted into the English language (see photo 10). At the time there was considerable alarm in the press that widespread damage might occur to forests around the world. Much research effort has been devoted into finding the causes of this tree dieback, and it is now evident that it is a very complex phenomenon. Air pollution and acid rain are certainly involved, and in some specific locations are the major culprit, but they are not the only factors. Acid rain can have serious effects on the leaves and needles of susceptible plants (and also damages some buildings!).

There is, however, now compelling evidence that soil pH in some parts of Europe decreased by as much as one whole unit in the last century. This does not sound much, but it actually means soil acidity has increased tenfold. Changes of this nature increase the toxicity of elements such as aluminium in the soil, and decrease the availability of some plant nutrients such as magnesium and calcium. It is hardly surprising that trees were found to be suffering so badly, but there were equally bad effects on lakes, which often lost their entire fish stocks.

Acid rain is now far less prominent in the news. Why is this? One reason is that the press reports of the 1980s were rather overhyped, and the damage to forests and other ecosystems has not been as bad as was predicted. A second is that the international community took firm action to combat the problem. Partly as a result of some thawing of relations between the East and the West, scientists and legislators from 34 nations, including the USA and Canada and many in Europe, were able to work towards an agreement to limit air pollution. On 13 November 1979 these nations signed the Convention on Long-Range Transboundary Air Pollution (LRTAP) in Geneva.[5] Further work led to agreement on the 1985 Sulphur Protocol, and there are now 50 parties to the Convention and a total of eight protocols.

The protocols gradually brought in targets to reduce emissions of a number of key pollutants across Europe and North America. Happily, **LRTAP** has been a major success, and in 25 years sulphur emissions across Europe have been decreased by 60%, and by almost half in the USA and Canada.[6] The clean-up job has been so successful that farmers in England are beginning to think about introducing sulphur into their fertilizer mixtures. Until recently their crops got all they needed from the sulphur-polluted rain! Nitrogen oxide emissions are still a problem, but are being steadily tackled. Funny, but apart from a few scientists, legislators and politicians nobody has heard of LRTAP. It certainly never gets mentioned in the press. Maybe it should, but then who wants to hear "good news"? It would not sell newspapers.

Every five years, scientists from around the world gather to discuss the latest research on acid rain. I was very pleased to attend the seventh such meeting, "Acid Rain 2005" in Prague, Czech Republic. This was a huge meeting with hundreds of delegates from every continent. The Czech Prime Minister, Jiří Paroubek, opened the conference, and it was soon evident that the Czechs took particular pride in their achievements on the pollution abatement front. The Czech Minister of the Environment, Libor Ambrozek, reported that the Republic had reduced its sulphur dioxide emissions by 87% in 2002 compared with 1990, nitrogen oxides by 57%, and greenhouse gases by 24.2%.

As is usual at such conferences, one day in the week was devoted to field trips. I had selected the trip to the Ore Mountains, north of Prague, and close to the Czech border with Germany. In the past, pollution from the power stations was so bad that it killed almost all the trees in the mountains. We visited the coal-fired station at Prunerov, and were shown the desulphurization plant. Now we could see how the Czechs had been so successful in reducing air pollution. Already the vegetation on the mountains was recovering, and new trees had been planted.

Overall the conference was incredibly positive, and almost everyone was very enthusiastic about the progress that had been made in combating acid rain, and about the future. There is just one small problem on the horizon: China. The Chinese are industrializing rapidly, and much of their economic growth depends on large numbers of coal-fired power stations being built. Their coal is high in sulphur, and their soils are very susceptible to acid rain. There was great speculation all week about where the next acid rain conference would be held in 2010. At the conference dinner we found out, when a member of the Chinese delegation, speaking on behalf of the Chinese Academy of Science, invited everyone to gather again in Beijing. Let us hope that the Chinese have the same drive and determination as the Czechs, and will be able to report major progress in 2010.

Great Tit eggs and acid rain

Andy Gosler is a zoologist in Oxford who is passionate about biodiversity and also about his Christian faith.[7] He told us a bit about the effects of acid rain on birds. His work on eggshell pigmentation shows that acid rain can have effects not just on plants and soils, but also on birds.

Andy writes: Like many other small passerines, Great Tits (*Parus major*) lay white eggs spotted with a reddish pigment (see photo 11). We have discovered that the purpose of these spots is to compensate for reduced eggshell strength when calcium is in short supply. This was shown, for example, by the fact that the pigment specifically marks thinner areas of shell.[8] Furthermore, we found that we could tell the actual eggshell thickness by the intensity of pigment spotting. Over the course of my study, the pigment patterns have changed, indicating that eggshells are now about 7% thinner than they were 20 years ago.[9]

Furthermore, this thinning effect seems to be greatest in birds nesting on limestone (rather than clay), and this seems to be because acid rain has leached calcium from the soil in those areas (repeat soil sampling shows that calcium content of the soil has declined most in limestone areas), so that there are now fewer snails there than there used to be.[10] So, amazingly, it is birds nesting on a huge calcium carbonate massif that have suffered the worst change in calcium availability due to acid rain, which still persists in central England.

Fall of creation

The interaction of people with the environment often has a harmful effect. As we found in Chapter 2, there is a delicate balance between our dominion or rule over the Earth and our responsibility for stewardship and care of creation. When the balance swings towards dominion the natural world suffers. We can trace this harmful impact through the Bible. In theological terms it is seen as "creation groaning". This is a New Testament term, found in Romans 8:22, but its origins can be found in the fall recorded in Genesis. Following the account of the creation of the world in Genesis 1, Genesis 2 portrays humans living in the idyllic Garden of Eden. Here they have everything they might possibly need easily at hand and are free to have an unimpeded relationship with God. No heavy toil was involved in this existence and people lived in perfect harmony with nature.

As well as the Garden, two other types of land are described in Genesis 2: "plain" or "field", which is thought to be uncultivated wilderness suitable for animal grazing, and dusty "land" or "ground", where agriculture is possible, with human effort and watering.[11] The Earth generally is described as being watered not by rain but by streams or springs, which came up from within the Earth (verses 5–6).

This could set the story in Mesopotamia, where farming was dependent on controlling the floodwaters of the Tigris and Euphrates. It is also reminiscent of the fertile lands of the Nile valley, but is a sharp contrast to the land of Canaan, which depends heavily on rainfall.

After the serpent tempted the woman to eat of the tree of the knowledge of good and evil, God brought judgement on the human race, and the rest of creation inevitably suffered from this. It has often been asked, "Why was seeking after this knowledge wrong?" Surely it is a good thing to know the difference between good and evil? One medieval scholar, Isaac Abravanel[12], explained that before the fall people must have had free will to be able to make the choice to disobey God. They must have also had intelligence, because they were made in the image of God and were given commands by God. He considered that the knowledge gained by eating from this tree was of a lower order: artificial human values that were in opposition to the natural existence God had provided. Eating of the tree symbolized material indulgence, a forsaking of living in harmony with nature, and an abandoning of the contemplation and acknowledgement of God, which is the true purpose of the human race.

The fall had a devastating effect on humankind. Adam and Eve were expelled from the garden and could now produce food only through painful toil. Eve bore two children: one became a keeper of flocks, while the other worked the soil. The name "Cain" comes from a Hebrew root that means "acquisition". He is rebuked for bringing an offering from the soil, which was cursed by God. Abel's name comes from the root word for "vanity". He seeks after the prestige of owning flocks, but finds favour with God for realizing the need for a blood sacrifice, and bringing some of the firstborn as an offering.[13]

Archaeologists have evidence that when our ancestors developed agriculture there was a significant rise in population (see Chapter 4). Once the change to agriculture had come about, a return to the previous hunter-gatherer existence was not possible for these communities because tending flocks and tilling the ground became the only means of sustaining one's family. As inequality arose between families, the two ambitions of wealth and status became driving forces for humankind. Later in Genesis we see Cain suffering the consequences of further sin. He was expelled from the fertile region and moved east of Eden, where he began to build a city. Ellul[14] points out that he was under the mark of God's protection, but by building his own settlement he had decided to trust in his own abilities to defend himself rather than trust in God's care.

The account of the fall does not only tell the story of the impact on humans of their disobedience to God; it also has significant things to say about the effect of this human sin on the whole of creation. Without people, nature would have continued in the perfect pre-fall condition in which God had created it. Once sin entered the world, the whole world was destined to suffer. This is partly a supernatural event: that is, creation had fallen and this state would have continued even if humans had been removed from the picture at that point. It was also, however, a result of the changing situation and activity of people. In this sense it is true to say that creation not only *fell*, but also began to be *felled* by human activities resulting from their changed circumstances. We can see this by looking at God's words to Adam in Genesis 3:17–19:

> To Adam he said, "Because you listened to your wife and ate from the tree about which I commanded you, 'You must not eat of it,'

"Cursed is the ground because of you, through painful toil you will eat of it all the days of your life. It will produce thorns and thistles for you, and you will eat of the plants of the field. By the sweat of your brow you will eat your food until you return to the ground, since from it you were taken; for dust you are and to dust you will return."

The supernatural element of the fall of creation is in verse 17. God has not cursed Adam, but instead the ground is cursed because of his sin. This is the land spoken about in Genesis 2:5–6, which can be cultivated and had been watered from underground springs. What does this curse mean? Does it mean that before the fall there was no death and decay?

Deuteronomy 33:13–16 speaks of God blessing land by sending "precious dew from heaven above and the deep waters that lie below" so that it will become exceptionally fertile. In the blessings for obedience in Deuteronomy 28:12, it states that God will "open the heavens, the storehouse of his bounty, to send rain on your land in season and to bless all the work of your hands". We can conclude that land that is blessed by God is well watered and fertile. It should follow, then, that the ground that is cursed is dry and lacking in fertility, and we can find this in the curses for disobedience in Deuteronomy 28:23: "The sky over your head will be bronze, the ground beneath you iron." This curse from God affected the natural ecological balance, so that the overabundance of nature in Eden was no longer the norm and landscapes with natural environmental stress came into existence. It was this stress that we saw highlighted in the passage from Hosea above.

We once spent a day with nomadic Bedouin in the Negev Desert in Israel (see photo 8). As we walked with them in a rocky desert region, we examined the plants adapted to the harsh arid environment. In the evening we sat around the campfire listening to their stories of the past. It was easy to imagine their ancestors telling the story of Genesis and dreaming of a time when this region might have been green and fertile. Even with today's technology it would prove impossible to permanently green the world's desert regions. Moreover, the predictions for this century are that vast areas of land where cultivation is now possible will become desert as our climate warms.

In our Earth there are many ecosystems, which experience natural environmental stress in the form of extremes of temperature, light or water. We can understand these environmental constraints as the core meaning of the curse on the ground in Genesis 3, and this can be compared to original sin, which was the result of the fall for our own species. The ideal of a sinless natural world would not be one where a decay cycle was non-existent, but would be a situation in which every ecosystem had an abundance of all its requirements for growth and completely lacked negative environmental stress.

Having examined the supernatural effects of the fall on creation, we need to consider the felling of creation by human activity. This could be categorized as a misuse of the gifts and responsibilities God gave to humans in the creation narratives. In the early chapters of Genesis we find accounts of agriculture, settlement and population growth. All these have the potential to develop in harmony with God's creation or to lead to the abuse of the natural world. Agriculture is highlighted in Genesis 3. In verse 18 Adam was commanded to eat the plants of the field, though their cultivation was now impeded by the introduction of thorns and thistles. Cassuto[15] links this back to Genesis 2:5. The term "plants of the field" is identical in each passage. These he identifies as barley and wheat, and this marks the beginning of grain cultivation. It was not so much that they were not in existence before but, lacking cultivation, they were scattered among other plants and not apparent as crops. The thorns and thistles, Cassuto suggests, are species coming under the heading of "shrub of the field", and these came into existence only with the fall of rain. It is interesting that these are weed species. Weeds occur only where humans have cultivated, since they are, by definition, unwanted plant species competing with the desired ones. There are no weeds in an untouched tropical rainforest, only the natural diversity of this ecosystem. When the forest is felled and a crop is planted, weeds are suddenly defined as any other plant trying to gain a foothold on the land that has been taken over by the farmer. Historically, the shrubs or weed species and the plants or grain species came into prominence with the emergence of agriculture, and this marked the beginning of the shaping of the natural world by humans.

This "shaping" inevitably had a diminishing effect on biodiversity. Mannion considered that agriculture "resulted in the partial control of energy flows, transformed biogeochemical cycles and biotas, set in train a massive extinction event that continues to impoverish the Earth's genetic resources and altered all Earth surface processes".[16] The consequence of the fall was that Adam and Eve had to leave their perfect garden and go into new environments that they needed to work and modify to sustain their expanding family. When our ancestors developed agricultural methods, their cultivation and urban development began to have a dramatic effect on the Earth. As population increased from hunter-gatherer times, so did human impact on the natural world.

Climate change

Acid rain is principally due to human-induced changes in the sulphur and nitrogen cycles, and can travel hundreds of miles before being deposited. In power stations, internal combustion engines and any other process that burns carbon compounds (in oil, gas, coal, wood, etc.), the gas carbon dioxide is produced. This gas is not washed out of the atmosphere to the same extent as sulphur dioxide and nitrogen oxides, and so it accumulates. It is the accumulation of carbon dioxide in our atmosphere worldwide that is the major (but not the only) driving force behind human-induced climate change.[17]

Carbon dioxide produced in one part of the world can diffuse to the rest of the planet's atmosphere, and is thus an example of global pollution. Since the beginning of the Industrial Revolution atmospheric carbon dioxide concentrations have increased from about 280 ppm to 379 ppm in 2005, and are continuing to increase every year. As we saw in Chapter 1, the greenhouse gases in our atmosphere are essential for keeping the planet at a reasonable temperature for life. However, increasing the amount of greenhouse gases in the atmosphere is like putting an extra blanket on a bed – it gets warmer in the bed! The best estimates suggest that global temperatures have increased by about 0.65°C in the last 130 years, with between 0.2 and 0.3°C of the increase occurring in the last 40 years. In 2007 the World Meteorological Organization[18] announced that all of the years since 2000 have ranked among the ten warmest years in the period ranging from 1850 to the present. Few of us will forget the very hot summer of 2003 in Europe. For those of you who have done a little statistics, that summer was five standard deviations away from the mean (millions to one against). Estimates vary, but it is thought to have caused about 35,000 deaths above the usual for that time of year. The worrying predictions are that the summer of 2003 will feel like an average summer in Europe by 2050, and it will be a cool summer by 2100. If we continue with "business as usual" and do nothing to reduce our carbon emissions, then carbon dioxide levels in the atmosphere could reach 650 ppm by 2100.

Of course, we very much hope that individuals, communities and governments will take action, and that such levels will not be reached. This is one of the snags in trying to predict future increases in temperature accurately, because we just do not know how much action will be taken, and when it will click in. In 2007, the Intergovernmental Panel on Climate Change (IPCC)[19] predicted that global mean surface temperature would probably rise by between 1.8°C and 4°C by 2100, with less likelihood of a rise between 1.1°C and 6.4°C. Even if the eventual change is in the lower part of this range, it will be unprecedented. The sceptics point out that changes in carbon dioxide levels and temperature have happened in the past. This is true, but it is the *rate* of change that has never been seen before. Of course, global averages conceal very great regional differences. These patterns are complex, but it appears likely that the developing nations of the world will suffer most from increases in temperature.

Temperature is not the only feature of the weather that is likely to change in the future. As it gets hotter there is more energy in the global weather system, and storms are predicted to become more frequent and heavier. There has been much debate in the press over whether Hurricane Katrina in 2005 was caused by climate change. The truth is that nobody can say whether any individual weather event was caused by increased temperature, but the overall probability of such events is increased. With Katrina, the sea surface temperature in the Gulf of Mexico was unusually high, and the hurricane passed directly over the hottest water. Inevitably, the energy from the water was transferred to the air above and the hurricane increased in strength as a result.[20] While some areas will see increased rainfall and storms, others are predicted to get drier and droughts will increase.

As the climate warms, sea level will rise, threatening the most low-lying areas of the world, mostly because water in the oceans will expand, but also due to melting ice caps and glaciers. The 2007 IPCC report suggested an average rise in sea levels globally of between 28 and 43 cm by 2100, but this excluded the melting of ice caps as the scientists were not yet confident that they could model this effectively. The very rapid changes in climate will probably mean that many organisms will not be able to adapt quickly enough, and decreased biodiversity will result (see Chapter 4). For humans, it will be the poor who will suffer most from climate change, whether they are the poor of Africa or the poor of New Orleans.[21] We will return to this in Chapter 9.

Before we leave the subject of climate change in this chapter it is important to deal briefly with the topic of climate scepticism. Although the number of sceptics seems to decrease every year, there are still some who deny that climate change is happening, or deny that humans are inducing it. They will often cite supposed disagreements between climate scientists to support their case. In fact, scientists almost universally support the story outlined above. Many hundreds of scientists from around the world have been involved in the IPCC reports, and there is unanimity on the key facts. In an attempt to provide quantitative evidence for this, Oreskes carried out a survey of the scientific literature between 1993 and 2003.[22] She searched on a database for papers containing the keywords "global climate change", and found 928. A quarter of these dealt with past climates or methods, and took no position on the debate. However, she considered that the remaining 75% all took the view that human induced climate change is happening. There has since been some criticism of the method used by Oreskes, as is usual in this area, but the overall conclusion stands. Certainly, our assessment of the academic climate scientists in the UK, both in Oxford and beyond, is that there are hardly any who do not hold the consensus view, and consider the matter very serious and urgent. So where does the idea of a "disagreement" come from? In his 2006 film and book *An Inconvenient Truth*[23] Al Gore reported that over half of newspaper articles displayed some scepticism about climate change. Gore implied that the source of many of the sceptical views was petrochemical giant ExxonMobil. In a totally unexpected and unusual move, the Royal Society, the most prestigious British scientific society, also criticized ExxonMobil for its financial support of organizations that give out misleading information on climate change.[24] ExxonMobil claimed that the Royal Society had "inaccurately and unfairly" described the company. Most recently, the Royal Society has produced a simple guide to the questions most commonly asked by climate sceptics.[25]

Where do we stand? Quite simply, we are convinced that human induced climate change is real, and needs our urgent attention at all levels: personal, community, regional, national and international. Climate change is a major challenge for humanity and needs to be tackled with the utmost urgency, and in Chapters 6–11 we will give some pointers on how to do it.

4

Standing room only for the creatures of the Earth

Can a Christian remain complacent about the issues of population? There is no room for complacency. Unless we want complete anarchy to rule the future world, we must contain population growth.

Sir Ghillean Prance, former director of the Royal Botanical Gardens at Kew[1]

One summer, I (Martin) gave a research seminar and visited a friend in Winnipeg, Manitoba, central Canada. At the airport when leaving I asked for, and was granted, a window seat not over the wing of the plane. I wanted to photograph the Great Plains (see photo 12). Soon after take off from Winnipeg the view was amazing, with miles and miles of incredibly flat agricultural land, stretching as far as could be seen. The Great Plains now mostly consist of numerous rectangular wheat fields, but once they were largely prairie. The very diverse grassland communities have been replaced by a monoculture of wheat. The reason for doing this was to provide food for the ever-growing human population. The two themes for this chapter are very much linked: increasing human population and decreasing biodiversity.

Go forth and multiply

Human population increase is undoubtedly one of the foremost environmental problems we are facing today. Humans require the basic necessities of food, shelter and warmth. The more people there are, the more of the Earth's surface area must be turned over to agriculture, the more houses are needed, the more fuel must be used, and the more methane and carbon dioxide are released into the atmosphere. All these activities have major environmental impacts, and so in very many ways human population growth is a root cause of environmental degradation.

When people were hunter-gatherers, and subject to very variable food supplies, the world human population was probably no more than a few million. People began to settle and farm the land about 10,000 years ago. One immediate effect of this was that food supplies became more predictable, and thus population began to rise, reaching about 250 million by 1 AD and 461 million by 1500.[2]

Humans differ from other species in their ability to plan for their future. Part of this planning involves concern for one's old age. At a time when infant mortality was very high it made sense to have a large family, as hopefully a few children would survive to maturity to look after their parents in old age. From our family tree, great-great-great grandfather Sampson Hodson, a farm labourer in Staffordshire, UK, married Elizabeth Woolams in Eccleshall in 1791. Sampson and Elizabeth went on to produce eight sons (no daughters!). Elizabeth apparently died soon after the birth of the eighth son, but Sampson lived on to the ripe old age of 86. Planning ahead certainly worked for Sampson – for well over 20 years he lived with the family of one of his sons in Eccleshall. His 86 year lifespan encompassed the beginning of the Industrial Revolution, and this period saw human population begin a period of rapid and sustained growth. By 1900 the world population stood at some 1.6 billion. The reasons for the continual increase in world population growth are complex, and well beyond the scope of this book, but better medical care, public health schemes and improved diet all contributed. In many societies birth rates remained high, but infant mortality decreased dramatically. The result was that the world population reached 2.5 billion in 1950, and 6 billion in 2000.[3]

We are in a rapid growth phase in human population, and there is a great deal of uncertainty about when this phase will stop. It is obvious to all that there must be some sort of upper limit to world population, but what is that limit? Technically, the maximum number of humans this planet can hold is called the "carrying capacity", and the key determinant in this is the food supply. Heilig[4] describes many estimates for carrying capacity, which are based on a variety of factors. The simplest models assume that economic, political, social and cultural restrictions on food production can be ignored, and that advanced agricultural technology will be available throughout the world. In these scenarios only physical and biochemical limitations are assumed to apply, and the estimates of maximum human population vary from 16 to 147 billion people.

However, these simplistic models almost certainly will not apply, and most experts suggest a figure that is at most two or three times bigger than our present world population, with a median figure of 10 billion.[5] Heilig concludes, "But could we also feed 10 to 15 billion people? Most likely, if we can prevent (civil) wars with soldiers plundering harvests or devastating crop fields with land mines; if we can stop the stupidity of collectivisation and central planning in agriculture; if we can agree on free (international) trade for agricultural products; if we can redistribute agricultural land to those that actually use it for production; if we provide credits, training, and high-yield seeds to poor farmers; if we can adapt the modern high-yield agriculture to the agro-climatic and sociocultural conditions of arid regions and use it carefully to avoid environmental destruction; if we can implement optimal water management and conservation practices. If we do all this during the next few decades, we would certainly be able to feed a doubled or tripled world population." As Heilig states, there are rather a lot of "ifs"!

What are the projections for human population growth in this century, and how do they compare with the carrying capacities suggested above? Long-range global projection is fraught with difficulties.[6] The first to attempt this was King in 1696, and his estimates of world populations of 630 million by 1950 and 780 million in 2050 have already proved to be gross underestimates. The medium projection by the United Nations is that human population will reach about 9 billion by 2054.[7] Beyond that date predictions become less and less certain, but we are likely to approach the maximum carrying capacity of the planet sometime during this century.

Global projections, however, hide some very real regional differences. In the developed West, population growth has slowed, and some countries now even have zero growth. Even in China population growth has slowed very considerably (see below). Again, the reasons for this slower growth are highly complex, and are certainly not fully understood. Large families are not nearly as common as was formerly the case. Low child mortality rates now mean that most children will survive to maturity, and the perceived need to produce large families has been taken away. The widespread adoption of birth control methods has enabled the timing of having children to be controlled. More women are embarking on careers, and are choosing to delay having children or not to have a family at all. The resulting decrease in population growth is not without its problems, however, and foremost among these is that of an ageing population. In "natural" populations, and throughout most of the developing world, there are large numbers of children, and relatively few elderly people. In the developed world, at least for a time, we will almost certainly have very large numbers of elderly people, and few children. The implications for social security, tax and pension systems are enormous.

The problems of the developed world are, however, very small indeed when compared to those of the developing (or Third) world. The Food and Agriculture Organization of the United Nations (FAO) estimated that 842 million people were undernourished in 1999 to 2001, with 798 million of those in developing countries.[8] The population explosion has outstripped food production in those areas, and is the cause of much environmental degradation and political instability.

To achieve a stable world population by the middle of this century we will need to achieve an average fertility rate of 1.7 children per woman. Unfortunately, the whole area of birth control is full of contentious issues for the church, and the Catholic Church, in particular, has campaigned vigorously against most methods of birth control. Governments are also facing very difficult problems, and the Chinese government came up with a radical, some would say draconian, solution to their population crisis.

In 1978 the Chinese population was already approaching one billion, and studies of land and water resources indicated that the carrying capacity of China was 1.2 billion.[9] So a campaign was launched in 1979 with the intention of persuading each family to have no more than one child. In return the families are given a number of benefits, such as free medical care and schooling for the one child. There are also financial penalties for couples breaking the rules. The scheme applies mainly to urban people and government employees, and has been less effective in rural areas. There are reports of couples deliberately taking fertility treatments to increase the chance of multiple births, and thus get around the law.[10]

However, overall the scheme has led to a considerable reduction in the Chinese birth rate.[11] Before the scheme started in 1979, Chinese women were having an average of 2.9 children each. In 2001, the average number of children for women over 35 was 1.94 and for women under 35 it was 1.73, which is below the replacement rate. Most women questioned wanted small families, with 92% preferring either one or two children. Younger women, those with better education, and those living in urban areas, tended to have smaller families. But one very large problem has emerged: a major imbalance in the sex ratio. The normal male to female ratio at birth is between 1.03 and 1.07, but in the period 1996–2001 the ratio in China had increased to 1.23. This almost certainly occurs mainly as a result of sex-selective abortion, but this is illegal and so it is impossible to obtain data. It is easy to criticize China for undertaking this massive exercise in social engineering, but very difficult to suggest realistic alternatives.

A filled Earth?

How do we reconcile the inevitable conclusion that we must limit population growth with the biblical command in Genesis 1:

> God blessed them and said to them, "Be fruitful and increase in number; fill the earth and subdue it."
> (Genesis 1:28)

One Genesis expert, Nehama Leibowitz[12], placed special emphasis on the detail of biblical descriptions, considering every letter and every word in the Bible to be significant.

She compared the description of the creation of people with that of fish and birds. Though fish and birds are told to be fruitful and increase in number, it is a general statement and therefore something they will do as a natural part of their existence. With people, Genesis records that God made his statement specifically "to them"; that is, God gives humans the conscious ability to multiply their numbers. We could therefore conclude that our ability to control our numbers is also God-given. There are, however, accounts in the Bible of people coming under judgement for limiting their fertility (see, for example, Genesis 38:9–10). How should we react to these? One perspective would be to compare the situation of the biblical characters with our position today. In biblical times world population was a fraction of its present figure, and there were vast stretches of fertile land available for our species to fill. If we have now filled the earth, could it be said that we have also fulfilled this commandment? If this is the case, the logical response is to limit the size of our families to play our part in helping to contain the population crisis. The leading Christian expert on human population, John Guillebaud, explains: "Some Christians believe that family planning, except by so-called natural methods, is always wrong; others that it is just permissible. I believe both groups are wrong. In my view, modern methods of birth control should be seen as a gift of God, both in helping many couples in their home lives, and in preventing a disaster of there being more people on the Earth than can live in harmony with God's creation."[13] Statistics show that most Christians in Western countries have already taken this route. Given that the greatest population rise is in non-Western countries, do we have a moral obligation to encourage those of other nations to reduce their families, and what are we prepared to do to help with the immediate negative consequences?

Peak Oil

Increased human population has put considerable pressure on the resources of the planet. In Chapter 3 we saw that increased burning of fossil fuels is leading to increased carbon dioxide in the atmosphere, a major driver for climate change. The other problem associated with fossil fuels is that they are a finite resource that will eventually run out. Of course we have known this for many years, but it is only recently that the concept of "Peak Oil", a much more urgent concern, has come to the fore. We asked an expert on Peak Oil, Dr Mike Pepler[14], to explain this idea:

Have we already reached Peak Oil? Energy is the ability to do work; it is used in everything we do, and comes from a variety of sources. The world of the 21st century is thoroughly dependent on oil and natural gas for a large portion of its energy needs. Gas is used for heating, industry, electricity generation and fertilizer production. Oil is used for transport, plastics, pesticides, medicines and much more.

When will the world run out of oil and gas? Not for hundreds of years – but this is the wrong question to ask. When will the world no longer be able to increase the production rate of oil and gas? Probably by 2010[15], if it hasn't reached this point already. The point at which production can no longer be increased is known as Peak Oil. Oil production in the USA peaked in 1970[16], as predicted by M. King Hubbert[17], the renowned Shell geologist. UK oil production peaked in 1999[18] and has recently been declining at around 10% per annum; UK gas production has also peaked, in 2000, and has been declining at around 5% per annum. Since the mid-1980s the world has been discovering less oil than it is using[19], and it is now only a matter of time before global production reaches its peak. After the peak, there is expected to be a plateau, followed by a decline of a few per cent every year. However, accidents, weather and politics can change all this without warning. We have huge amounts of infrastructure dependent on oil and gas, and it will take a long time to rebuild them. The time to start is already long gone, but if we act fast the problems can be mitigated. The consequences of not acting will be disastrous.

Peak Oil has been discussed by some environmentalists for some time, but it would be true to say that it has not yet made anything like the same impact as climate change on the public. Many books on climate change do not even consider it. However, all this may be changing, and since Mike wrote his piece above, I (Martin) have spotted an article in the top American journal *Science*. Entitled "Even oil optimists expect energy demand to outstrip supply", the article gave an overview of several recent reports, some suggesting that maximum oil production will happen by 2010, as Mike suggests.[20]

Habitat and biodiversity loss

One of the major impacts of population growth has been a decrease in natural habitats, caused either by our increased agricultural activities or by urban sprawl. According to the Millennium Ecosystem Assessment,[21] agriculture now accounts for about 25% of Earth's land surface. Between 1950 and 1980 more land was converted to cropland than between 1700 and 1850. Agricultural practices had led to the degradation of 562 million hectares of cropland worldwide by 1990, about 38% of the roughly 1.5 billion hectares total.[22]

Following on behind changes to agricultural use comes the threat from urban development. Put simply, once soil has been built on it is almost impossible to restore the land to its original state, and it is lost for good. What are the trends? The amount of the Earth's land surface dedicated to urban uses is just 1% of the total, but this is growing rapidly.[23] In the United States, urban population growth has slowed to less than 1.3% per year but urban sprawl has continued, and land dedicated to urban uses increased from 21 to 26 million hectares between 1982 and 1992.

Tropical rainforests

One of the most publicized examples of loss of habitat is that of the tropical rainforests, and there are an abundance of gloomy figures and predictions. In Chapter 2 we highlighted that these are biodiversity hotspots and are especially rich in species. Over half of the world's tropical rainforests have already been removed, the rate of deforestation was at the highest ever recorded in the 1980s and 1990s, and the rate is continuing to increase in some areas.[24] The forests are often logged for their valuable hardwoods, and then turned over to farming. Unfortunately, some of the rainforest soils are not suitable for agriculture, as they are frequently surprisingly infertile. In many cases most of the mineral nutrients in a tropical rainforest are locked up in the trees, and the soils often contain very little. The soils are vulnerable to erosion, and may be severely damaged. In some areas quite large amounts of land are eventually taken over by secondary forest, as agriculture is abandoned. Animal species diversity can recover in these forests within 20–40 years, but secondary forests have fewer tree species than the original forest. Large areas of virgin tropical forest now have government protection, but it is likely that these areas will become islands surrounded by agricultural land and secondary forest. It is uncertain what level of biodiversity will remain in such a situation. Loss of forests also leads to increases in atmospheric carbon dioxide due to the burning of forests and soils, and to decreases in absorption of carbon dioxide by photosynthesis due to lack of trees.

Lewis[25] has painted a depressing future scenario for our tropical rainforests. Instead of being net sinks for carbon dioxide, absorbing more from the air than is released back, they could become net sources of carbon dioxide through four major processes:

a) photosynthesis declining and respiration increasing due to increased temperatures caused by climate change;

b) biodiversity changes in the remaining forests, with faster growing species which have a lower carbon content becoming dominant;

c) droughts induced by climate change causing extensive forest breakdown;

d) increased fires caused, in part, by the drier climate.

So climate change could have a serious impact on the remaining tropical forests, which of course would lead to even further losses of biodiversity. We can clearly see here that environmental issues that are frequently put into separate "boxes", climate change and biodiversity, in fact interact rather more than we might expect.

Urban sprawl

In the developed West we have a tendency to see habitat destruction as largely a problem for the developing world. With our better environmental legislation and vigorous green lobby, surely we have fewer problems? Unfortunately, this is not the case. In the United Kingdom, the Environment Agency[26] suggested that in 2000 about 10% of the land in England and Wales was in urban use. This figure has grown rapidly in the last 50 years. Between 1985 and 1996 there was a net change to developed use of around 7,200 hectares of land a year in England. It is predicted that, by 2016, around 12% of England and Wales will be urbanized. In the UK in the last 50 years of the 20th century, over half of the remaining ancient woodland was lost. Half of England's heaths have been lost since 1950, and similar figures could be quoted for grasslands and fens. About 70% of European coastlines are highly threatened, and, between 1965 and 1995, a kilometre of European coastline was developed every day.[27]

It may seem obvious that land will be most under threat from urban development in areas of the world where population is rising rapidly – the more people, the more houses will be needed. Then why is it that urban development seems to continue even in countries, such as the UK, where population growth has slowed or even reversed? It seems we need more houses with fewer people living in them. Keilman[28] reported that in 1950 a typical house in the developed world had about 3.5 occupants, but by 2000 this number had fallen to 2.5. The reasons for this are complex, but include increased individual freedom, women having greater economic independence, fewer households of extended families, and higher divorce rates. Therefore, we build more houses and permanently lose more land and habitat.

Biodiversity loss

Loss of habitat is one of the main reasons for loss of biodiversity. Not only are there fewer animals or plants of a particular species, but also there are fewer species.[29] Plants and animals have always been becoming extinct and it is a totally natural process. There is, however, no doubt that the present extinction spasm is very large, and probably bigger than any other in the geological record. We know that some 654 plant and 535 animal species have become extinct since 1600.[30] These figures are almost certainly vast underestimates. Just saying when a species is extinct is often a very difficult problem. Many species, maybe 80–90% of the total, have yet to be named and described, and so could become extinct without our knowing. Even now some species of large animals are still being discovered, and between 1990 and 2002 scientists have described 24 monkeys that are new to science, thirteen from Brazil alone.[31] In 2006, there were several reports in the news of new species of shark being discovered, including two "walking" sharks from Indonesia, a new Mustelus shark from the Sea of Cortez off Mexico, and a new hammerhead shark off South Carolina.[32]

If we do not know all of the large animals on the planet, then the extinction of smaller species, such as insects, may go totally unnoticed. One of the most famous recent extinctions was that of the passenger pigeon in 1914. It is less well known that two species of lice that lived only on this pigeon became extinct at the same time. This example illustrates one of the problems of extinction – if one animal or plant becomes extinct, and it provides a food source or other benefit for another, then a whole cycle of extinctions may set in. Current estimates are that about 24% of the world's mammals and 11% of its birds are threatened with extinction.[33] It is not simply the declining numbers of species but the plummeting size of the wild animal population worldwide. Researchers in Vienna have calculated that only 3% of all vertebrate animal flesh is wild.[34] This means that 97% is made up of either humans or our domestic animals. This stark figure sums up the wildlife crisis that we face.

Great Tit eggs and climate change

In most cases, climate change has negative impacts on bio-diversity, but occasionally there are positive effects, at least for a time.

Andy Gosler[35] writes: For the past 25 years I have studied Great Tits (*Parus major*) in Wytham Woods as part of a long-term population study of this species, started in 1947 and run by the Edward Grey Institute of Field Ornithology (see photo 11). Over the course of this study we have seen a number of important changes in the pattern of breeding, which are related to the warming climate. The birds' breeding season typically runs from April to June, and when we were planning for *my* first such season, my boss Chris Perrins told me that so long as I was back from my Easter break by 20 April, I shouldn't have missed anything. In other words none of the birds should have started laying eggs by then. These days, because of higher spring temperatures, the breeding season has moved back, so that since 1990, all the birds are incubating by 20 April. If we didn't start until 20 April these days, we'd have missed the laying period and would be uncertain when the first eggs were laid (which is critically important for us). In fact so much earlier are they nowadays that most birds can delay incubation after completing their clutch (they lay one egg each day until it is complete), so as to time the brood's hatching to make best use of the short-term flush in the tree-defoliating caterpillars that occurs in May. This means that all eggs are incubated together, and so hatch more or less simultaneously. Before about 1990, many birds started incubation before the clutch was complete, which resulted in a few chicks hatching 1–3 days later than the rest of the brood, and these late chicks often died. So a warmer spring seems to be beneficial.[36]

Creation in bondage

Christians looking for biblical guidance to explain environmental problems and suggest solutions have frequently turned to Romans 8:19–22:

> The creation waits in eager expectation for the sons of God to be revealed. For the creation was subjected to frustration, not by its own choice, but by the will of the

one who subjected it, in hope that the creation itself will be liberated from its bondage to decay and brought into the glorious freedom of the children of God. We know that the whole creation has been groaning as in the pains of childbirth right up to the present time.

This is the only major New Testament reference to creation[37] and it is easy to see this passage in terms of the environmental problems of today. It seems to speak so clearly into the situation of landscapes under stress, as we have seen in this and the previous chapter. However, we need to also interact with the Romans themselves; how would they have seen this passage? They would never have heard of global warming, acid rain or the population crisis. So what was Paul thinking in this passage and what would the Romans have understood from it? We can be sure that many of the Christians in Rome would have been well versed in the Old Testament, and also in what we would now call apocryphal writings. Meyer[38] considers that the Romans would have based their thinking on "the firm understanding of the affinity between human beings and God's total creation, of which they are a part, that runs through the Old Testament and the apocryphal literature". Although we are made in the image of God, we are part of creation, not separate from it. As a part of the natural world we are subjected to the bondage of death and decay, we are subjected to disease, and are vulnerable to natural disasters. From the other point of view, creation has the human species to contend with as part of its structure. We have seen that the fall of Adam and Eve affected not only people, but all creation. For this reason, the whole of nature is under strain and continues to "groan". The natural world had no choice in this, because it came as a result of God's judgement on humanity. In this sense the passage may be referring to the created order apart from people.

The key purpose of this passage is to look not to the past, but to the future. The New Testament brings us good news: Jesus, in dying to redeem us from our sin, has achieved something so universal that he has also made possible the redemption of the natural world. The frustration of creation is only transitory, and soon there will be glorious freedom for the whole earth. Here we clearly see the influence of Hebraic thought, in which ideas of the renewal of creation are frequently linked to God's end time redemption in the Bible. Joel 3:18 is an example and speaks of the end of the age when nature will be abundantly fruitful:

> In that day the mountains will drip new wine,
> and the hills will flow with milk;
> all the ravines of Judah will run with water.
> A fountain will flow out of the LORD's house
> and will water the valley of acacias.

This concept of end times redemption is also apparent in the imagery of a woman in childbirth used in Romans 8:22. The pangs of childbirth would have been seen as illustrations of the cosmic woes accompanying God's judgement, and they are a metaphor here for the universally shared pain that looks forward to new life. What we believe will eventually happen to the Earth at the end of the age has an effect on our attitude to the natural world today.

Creation groaning in Romans takes us beyond the problems resulting from the fall, and looks towards the redemption of the natural world at the end times. Though there are other biblical passages speaking of a renewed earth (e.g. Isaiah 65:17 and Revelation 21:1), this passage foresees renewal in terms of liberation. We will return to these passages in Chapter 11, where we will take a hopeful look at the future of the Earth and see how this should affect our actions today.

Conclusion

In October 2007, the United Nations Environment Programme (UNEP) released GEO-4, which covers both of the major topics addressed in the present chapter.[39] On human population they conclude: "As a result of the growing competition and demand for global resources, the world's population has reached a stage where the amount of resources needed to sustain it exceeds what is available." On biodiversity loss UNEP were equally forthright: "All available evidence points to a sixth major extinction event currently underway. Unlike the previous five events, which were due to natural disasters and planetary change, the current loss of biodiversity is mainly due to human activities."

We have seen that the Earth God made, which was described in Chapters 1 and 2, has been seriously damaged (Chapters 3 and 4). The root cause of the problem appears to be spiralling human population growth, which is a major contributor to both climate change and biodiversity loss. Space has not permitted us to look at other very serious environmental problems: soil erosion; water shortages, infectious diseases, etc. We have also seen that human sin and greed have been major factors. In Chapter 5 we will unpack this idea a little more, as we look at how the church has responded to environmental issues in the past. Then in Chapters 6–11 we will concentrate on how Christians and others are attempting to solve the environmental crisis we find ourselves in.

5

The seeds of history

"I don't think God is going to ask us how he created the earth, but he will ask us what we did with what he created."

Revd Richard Cizik, vice-president of governmental affairs for the National Association of Evangelicals[1]

La Verna is desolate and beautiful. Perched on a rugged mountainside above precipitous ravines, it is a place to hear birdsong and the wind rustling through the trees. If you stay still long enough you will see small mammals and glimpse deer moving through the forest. Deep in the mountains north of Arezzo in Italy, it is easy to see why St Francis chose it as his mountain hideaway. This was the place where he had some of his most profound experiences of God.

Christians throughout history have found natural places to be settings where they could meet with God following the biblical model of the Exodus, the inspiration of the Psalms, and Jesus' pattern of prayer. It seems strange, then, that there has not been a consistently positive approach to nature by Christians. To understand this we need to look at how different historical groups of Christians have viewed the natural world in relation to their faith and salvation.

The early church

Jesus came from the countryside, and we have seen already that his teaching fits into a rural context (Chapter 2). In contrast, the first Christians were mostly urban, and contemporary issues of how to relate to the land and to animals were not greatly relevant. The early church saw the Old Testament as their scriptures and the emerging New Testament as scripture that was explaining and developing these earlier books. Since there was already a very comprehensive guide to how we should approach nature in the Old Testament, there was little to add. What they did write about was how the gospel affected the cosmic status of the rest of nature, so passages such as Romans 8:18 and Revelation 22 gave insight into God's desire to end the bondage of the earth to decay and liberate his creation as a new heaven and Earth. They also explored the cosmic implications of Christ's divinity, and passages such as John 1:1–4 and Colossians 1:15–20 reveal Christ's role as both creator and sustainer of the universe. We looked at Romans 8 in Chapter 3 and will consider these passages further in Chapter 11.

The majority of the next generation of Christians were from a Greek background and many were influenced by the Neo-Platonic idea of a dualism between body and soul. The Persian philosopher Mani (210–276) also influenced Christians, including Augustine (354–430). Mani believed in a dualism between good and evil. Both these views tended to lead to a negative view of the material world. Some people who were initially drawn to Christianity were so influenced by these dualistic views that they eventually drifted into Gnosticism. Gnostics believed in a higher god who presided over the spiritual realms and a lesser, imperfect, god who presided over the material realms. These views were rightly seen as inconsistent with the Christian faith.

The Old Testament taught a distinction between God and creation and also between humanity and the rest of creation. It did not take a negative view of this world because it was seen as lovingly created by God. Despite Greek influences, this positive biblical view was reflected in the creeds, which affirmed a creator God (the Greeks believed in an eternal universe), the physical incarnation, and a bodily resurrection of Jesus. Throughout history, however, many Christians have tended to confuse a biblical distinction between God and creation with the Greek and Persian dualisms.

The Western church, Augustine, Benedict and Francis

The two strands of a positive biblical view of the natural world and a negative view of matter as evil wove through the pages of Christian history. They are most evident and interwoven in the Western church. St Augustine's writings reveal both these views. He drew extensively on natural images in developing his theology, and showed sensitivity to nature as something that is God-given. At the same time, he saw physical desires and other aspects of the material world as factors that could draw the believer away from the true worship of God and realization of their salvation. Much of his writings concern his own personal struggle to find salvation, and the material world was frequently seen as a distraction from this goal.[2]

St Benedict (480–447) had an appreciation of God's creation as a means for aiding human salvation, and worked his faith out through a concept of community. He developed a rule of living, whereby his monks had to commit themselves to living in one community for life and so be rooted in one place. Each monastery had to be self-sufficient, living off the produce of its land. Benedictines took a sacramental approach to farming the land, and were deeply aware of the link between the fruits of the earth and of the elements of communion. They saw working the land as engaging with God's creation, and therefore a spiritual act of service.[3]

Much has been written about St Francis and a Christian appreciation of nature. Francis (1182–1226) sought wilderness to meet with God, and had an unusual affinity with animals. What is less often highlighted is his intense awareness of evil in the world, and his struggle with evil forces even in the wilderness paradise of places such as La Verna. This could be seen as a dualistic view that might have led to a negative view of nature. In fact, St Francis' dualism is conceived as between good and evil, rather than between the material and the spiritual. This means that his theology was able to embrace a positive view of nature, while still being very aware of the evil forces affecting our world. He saw God's salvation as for the whole of creation, and not just for humans. Legends speak of him preaching to birds and taming wolves. The example of St Francis as a lover of nature, and prayers such as his "Canticle to the Sun", still inspire many Christians who seek a more ecological approach to their faith.

Eastern Orthodox Church

The Orthodox churches in the Middle East and Eastern Europe remained more strongly influenced by a positive view of creation.[4] As their theology developed they placed a particular emphasis on the incarnation of Christ. As Jesus is eternally begotten of the Father, so the role of creator is an eternal characteristic of the Trinity.[5] In other words, creating a material universe was not simply a bright idea that God had, but was a natural outworking of the character of our God. The zenith of this creativity was the birth of Christ – truly the crown of all creation. God, who was invisible, was now fully with us in a material sense. This view of God and of creation led Eastern Orthodox Christians to view the world around them as something very precious that God had made, and which he had sanctified through the incarnation. The practical response to this theology was (and still is) a respectful approach towards the natural world.[6]

Celtic Christians

The Celtic church flourished in the British Isles during the early medieval period, (roughly from 400 to 900 AD). It was distinct from the Western church, and partly drew on the theology and practice of the Eastern Christian traditions.[7] Celtic Christians saw God's presence and divine power revealed in nature.[8] They believed the Earth to be hallowed through the birth of Christ and still the dwelling place of God through his Holy Spirit. This understanding of the presence of God led them to a vivid appreciation of the natural world. Wild places and nature were so important to St David that he would recite the Psalms while standing in a lake up to his neck in cold water.[9] As he got closer to God's creation so he found access to the presence of God himself. This highly developed idea of the importance of wilderness as a place to meet with God led Celtic Christians to seek out places of natural interest to found their religious communities. They lived a life committed to simplicity and living in harmony with God's world around them. There was a strong emphasis on geographical place, with a belief in the sacredness of certain places, such as holy wells and holy islands.

This awareness of the immanence of God did not lead to a withdrawal from the world, however, but to an affirmation of it. The monasteries founded by the Celtic monks were farming communities that, like their Old Testament forebears, saw the spiritual life as something to be worked out in practical management of the land. Though they met God in the wilderness, they served God in a pastoral setting. Their communities may seem remote to our modern world, but in the Celtic era they became centres of cultural life and were well connected to other Celtic settlements, usually by boat. This was the main mode of transport for a country that had not been cleared of its forests. It was the interior of Britain that was remote, and not its coastline and islands. Celtic monks lived close to nature, by manual labour, in a community life of prayer. It was this lifestyle that enabled them to encounter God and share their faith with others as they were connected to other parts of the world.

If Celtic Christians saw the wilderness as deeply spiritual, they did not have a romanticized view of nature. They were alive to the unpredictable ferocity and terror of the natural world, and prayed for protection within it. The dangers and perils of nature, and indeed death itself, were seen as part of the whole and not something that was separate. God's providence permeated the whole of life and the whole earth, and those who trusted God had to hold to that trust through choppy waters of pain and suffering, as well as in the blessings of life that brought wonder, love and joy.[10]

Views on the purpose of creation

One of the key debates that affected the treatment of nature by humans has been discussion of the purpose of creation. The concept that creation was for human benefit alone can be found in the medieval writings of Christianity, Judaism and Islam. In the medieval understanding of this view, the Earth was seen as providentially filled with the good things that humans needed for existence. The role of humans was to live within this fruitful world, and benefit from it through their daily work. So, although this was an anthropocentric approach, it was not incompatible with a biblical stewardship principle.

It was not the only medieval view, however. The great Jewish philosopher Moses Maimonides (1135–1204), came up with a different, but very biblical answer.[11] A doctor and a community rabbi, Maimonides had every reason to put humans centre stage. He could not forget the rest of creation, however, and believed in the intrinsic value of all nature. He argued from the basis that not all of creation was required for human benefit, and therefore it must have been created for some other purpose. Since God did not need to create a universe for his own personal fulfilment, Maimonides concluded that all of nature was created simply as a result of God's will. Creation was therefore made for the glory of God. In his most famous book, *The Guide for the Perplexed*, he wrote: "The universe does not exist for man's sake but each being exists for its own sake, and not because of some other thing."[12] His *Guide* was read widely by Christians in the Middle Ages, including Thomas Aquinas, and may have influenced some who subsequently took a respectful view of nature. It did not become the dominant view, however, and this was partly because of a rise of a very different philosophy in the Renaissance.

The Renaissance and human supremacy

The Renaissance flourished in Europe from the 15th century and played a key role in changing the perception of the relationship between humans and the Earth.[13] It was a period of cultural self-confidence when the magnificence of humanity was celebrated. In this period the term "humanist" did not mean someone who lacked a religious faith, but rather someone who believed in the supreme dignity of humans and their potential for achievement. In the Renaissance people frequently looked back to the achievements of the Classical World and sought to build on them. There were many positive outcomes from this attitude, such as the blossoming of the arts and sciences, but there was also a negative outcome in the conclusions drawn concerning the human relationship to nature. The problem came from the combination of the belief that humans had supreme potential, with the view that everything in the material world was made for human benefit. If human creativity could change and shape the Earth, which they believed was for them alone, then it was logical to conclude that humanity could rightfully dominate all other creatures on Earth, and do with them as it willed.

Creation began to be seen as something deliberately created to be raw and incomplete, waiting for humans to take it and refashion it into something much better. These ideas permeated to the heart of Christian Europe, and many Christians discarded the biblical stewardship ethic. It was replaced with a progressive idea of free dominion that would lead humans to believe that they could and should create a "better world" for them to live in.

The purpose of science

This combination of biblical and Greek ideas meant that the stage was set for the development of modern science and technology. There are some who have argued that it set it in a way that would ultimately prove hazardous to the Earth.[14] The Scientific Revolution would open the way for the huge modern advances in understanding our world, and give humanity vastly increased potential to change it, either for better or for worse.

This potential for change was not new: humans may have begun to influence the Earth's climate, for example, when they started to clear the forests of the Mediterranean and Eurasia around 8,000 years ago and released their carbon into the atmosphere. The ancient Chinese first domesticated rice about 10,000 years ago. Cultivation of rice in paddy fields came later and spread across the Far East from about 5,000 years ago. This method of growing increased the methane levels in the atmosphere. Methane is a greenhouse gas, and it has been suggested that the domestication of rice had a global warming impact.[15] Bill Ruddiman, a leading paleoclimatologist, proposes that these human activities prevented the global climate from following its natural cycle and going into a new ice age, which was due for our own era.[16] Not all agree with this theory but it is widely accepted as a possibility, and has led to the term "Anthropocene" being coined to describe our present geological epoch.[17]

This example helps to show that the development of modern science and technology were not in themselves the cause of our current environmental crisis. Significant impacts on the environment had been happening for thousands of years already. The difference has been the speeding up of the rate of change, especially with the onset of the Industrial Revolution.

Francis Bacon (1561–1626) was committed to the idea of scientific progress based on a more progressive understanding of scientific method, which involved experimentation rather than simply observation. He believed that the goal of science was to gain dominion over nature by understanding it and so to be able to use it for human benefit. This was an ideal that has led to many, if not all, scientific advances that have aided humanity. Modern medicine and technology are a result of this ethos, and few people would refuse the benefits that these advances offer. The downside came when this view became welded together with human greed, and a complete lack of a sense of limits to the use of the rest of nature for humans. This distorted the Renaissance ideal of creating a better world for all, and denied the biblical idea of caring for the Earth as something God-given.

The approach of Francis Bacon was not the sole way in which nature was viewed by scientists of this period. John Ray (1627–1705) was an eminent biologist and one of the founders of the Royal Society. He believed that all living creatures were made for themselves and to glorify God. He saw nature as a second revelation of God, a "book of works" that complemented the Bible, God's book of words. Ray's scientific endeavours therefore had a spiritual dimension to them. He has been described as the father of modern botany. Ray provided the foundation for much later work, including an early method of classifying plants and animals.[18] William Derham (1657–1735) also took up the theme of stewardship, and reminded fellow scientists that we had been given this world in trust, and would one day be called to account.[19]

The purpose of science, therefore, as conceived during the Scientific Revolution, was not to plunder nature but to study nature; not to destroy the world for profit but to seek to improve the world for human habitation. All these ends were, in themselves, sustainable, and all were compatible with the biblical world view from which they sprang. Damage occurred when the powerful tools that science and technology developed were used for personal gain regardless of the impact their use would have on the powerless – whether people or planet.

Darwin and debates on creation and evolution

Biblical faith is based on the concept of a universe that has an origin, and of a progression of history from the beginning of the world, through the salvation in Christ,

and onwards towards our final redemption and the reconciliation of all things. This gave it a sense of ultimate origins of all things and an idea of progression through time.
It is not surprising that this world view provided the intellectual atmosphere that allowed scientists to question the
origin and development of the universe, and also to investigate the origins and progression of life on Earth.

John Ray and William Derham were both supporters of
the concept of "Natural Theology", the idea that it is possible to learn more of God through the study of his world.
This idea has a biblical basis: for example, in Romans 1:20
St Paul argues that God's power and his divine nature have
been clearly revealed in nature.[20] William Paley
(1743–1805) took this concept to its furthest end point. In
1802 he published his work *Natural Theology*, in which he
gave numerous examples of God's benevolent will revealed
in nature, and particularly in the animal kingdom.

Paley coined the idea of comparing the universe to a
carefully constructed watch, therefore "proving" the existence of God as the necessary watchmaker. The danger of
this work was that the detail of his explanations came to be
seen by some as "the" proof of God's existence. Any proof
of God that depends on gaps in scientific knowledge is vulnerable to those gaps being filled by natural explanations.
The young Charles Darwin (1809–1882) read Paley's book,
and his copy is annotated with his own notes, which frequently questioned Paley's conclusions. His common
ground with Paley was his fascination with the diversity of
species and his desire to search out a rational explanation.

When *The Origin of Species* was published in 1859, it
was not (as is sometimes suggested) met with dismay by
the church. Those who were committed to the watchmaker
view were opposed, but many Christians embraced
Darwin's views and found them consistent with a Christian

belief in a creator God. Victorian clergyman Charles Kingsley wrote to Darwin to encourage him in his theory of the Origin of Species, explaining that for God to create the world in such a way that organisms could make themselves is far cleverer (than the watchmaker concept). It is, in fact, far more consistent with the biblical view of a creator God working through creation and through history. The static view of a one-off creative act by a watchmaker has its philosophical origins in Enlightenment deism, because it sees God as someone who stands outside his creation rather than being involved with it. Kingsley's view became popular among Christians, especially in Britain, and is known as "theistic evolution". This accepted the evolutionary process as something God-given and saw it as entirely consistent with the revelation of the Bible. There were, of course, other views.

If the Judaeo-Christian world view had had an influence on science, the scientific approach had also affected the way Christians viewed their faith, and this was particularly evident in the way that scripture was viewed and interpreted. Before the Reformation, the Bible was primarily viewed allegorically. Many of the descriptions of nature were basically seen as metaphors for aspects of the human condition before God. The Reformation was based on a more rational and objective approach to the Bible, and texts were now interpreted according to their straightforward meaning.

As the scientific revolution advanced, so this rational response to scripture developed into a scientific interpretation. If the natural world could reveal the hand of God through objective empirical study, so the Bible could reveal how God acted in scientific terms. An understanding of the Genesis texts on creation thus shifted from a pre-modern view of an account that stood alongside actual history and explained it theologically, to seeing them as literal historical descriptions that would provide information for scientific discovery. Those who followed this line of thinking rejected Darwin and the development of evolution, and believed in a literal seven-day creation as seven 24-hour periods. Many devout Christians who were and are very good scientists have held to this view. They do so by not trying to align their scientific understanding with biblical revelation. Others became "scientific creationists", seeking to use science to prove this particular view of Genesis. Moving into the 20th century, there were two "middle-way" developments. The first was "ancient creationism". This accepted the vast evidence of geology for an ancient Earth, but still held to a seven-day creative act. The second, more recent, development has come in reaction to the growing evidence of biological evolution. This is the "intelligent design" (ID) school of thought. As with theistic evolution, followers of this accept the biological evolutionary process as well as a geological timescale. It differs significantly from theistic evolution in believing that some aspects of our world have come from specific intervention by God to cause the evolutionary process to go in the direction of his purposes. Therefore an ID person believes that sometimes evolution is "by chance" but at other times it is through "intelligent design". A theistic evolutionist would differ in believing that the universe, on inception, was charged with all the potential to evolve life according to God's providence. It had the presence of God throughout time, sustaining the universe, while his purposes have been gradually revealed. If God has been present and active in his universe, he has not, however, needed to intervene to move evolution along – all the potential for that was there from the start and could have come about from a myriad of different evolutionary pathways.

Creation and environmental concern

Readers of this book will take different views on the creation/evolution debate. As authors, we have inevitably been more sympathetic to our own view of theistic evolution, and some may wish to challenge this! It is important, however, to focus on the key purpose of this book, and ask, "Will different views of the origins of life affect the way we cherish the Earth today?" All Christians, whatever their views on origins, will concede that our Earth originates with God and is rightfully his. Those who hold strictly to creationism should avoid using it as a reason for a Christian withdrawal from science and concern about the environment. Likewise, those who take an evolutionary approach should be cautious of an overly optimistic belief in science and technology to overcome environmental problems. Whether a person believes the universe came into being in seven days a little over 6,000[21] years ago or has evolved over millions of years, each Christian still needs to take seriously the Psalmist's words, "The Earth is the Lord's and everything in it" (Psalm 24:1). The command to care for the Earth therefore transcends views on creation and evolution. These may affect how we understand our current environmental predicament (for example, much of the past climate change data depends on an acceptance of geological time), but it will not affect the overwhelming evidence that we have major environmental problems in our world today. As Isaiah states, "The earth is defiled by its people, they have disobeyed the laws, violated the statutes and broken the everlasting covenant".[22] Our conclusion about creation and evolution is that we need to set aside our differences in what we believe about origins, and instead put our energies into acting responsibly and in a biblical way towards our planet today.

The rise of the environmental movement

We have moved from older Christian approaches to the Earth through to a brief summary of the interrelation of science and faith after the Renaissance, and considered the influence each has had on the other. Alongside this cultural progression was the gradual build up of environmental problems worldwide. By the 1960s these were becoming a cause for concern. Rachel Carson's book *Silent Spring* was published in 1962, and focused a generation on the devastating effects of modern lifestyle. These concerns stimulated a philosophical search for the cause of this ecological crisis. In the atmosphere of the 1960s, Christianity was an easy target.

In the UK there remained a strong link between science and Christianity, and a surprisingly high proportion of scientists were also practising Christians. The overlap was possibly less strong elsewhere, especially in the United States, where a much stronger adherence to seven-day creationism had led to a tendency for Christians to avoid scientific disciplines and to study something "safer" for their faith. At the same time, within the church, Christian missionary endeavour was fairly divided into two camps, with more liberal Christians promoting a "social gospel" of human care, and more evangelical Christians focusing on proclamation and conversion. Neither had a major focus on the environment.

It was into this scenario that, in 1967, Lynn White published his famous essay in the prestigious journal *Science*, laying the blame for the current ecological crisis firmly on Christianity.[23] White's essay provoked a steady stream of responses at academic and popular level. It is now widely agreed that his thesis was flawed, though it still plays a role in popular thinking in the green movement, which can caricature Christianity as a "non-green" faith. In the spirit of the 1960s many Westerners were turning to the religions of the East. The combination of meditative asceticism and simple lifestyles provided an attractive alternative for those who were seeking a spiritual way of living, but had rejected the Christianity of their parents. As with the more platonic forms of Christianity, the philosophical shortcoming of some of the popular movements was the classic dualism between the spiritual and material. Many strands of this 1960s spirituality taught a simple lifestyle and spiritual encounter, with an ultimate aim of escaping this world for true fulfilment elsewhere. This led to living a very green lifestyle, but it did not really provide a very positive view of the Earth.

The Eastern approaches developed philosophically, with theories such as Deep Ecology, proposed by Arne Næss in 1973.[24] This theory proposed that humans are an integral part of their environment, and emphasized the interconnectedness of all aspects of our world and universe. It is deeply ecocentric, considering humans to be alongside other creatures as equals.

At the same time, a British scientist was exploring the concept of scientific feedback mechanisms on a global scale. In 1972 James Lovelock published his first paper on the Gaia hypothesis,[25] proposing that we should treat the Earth as a single organism. Lovelock believed that the Earth was able to maintain its own homeostasis, or equilibrium, because a change in one aspect would stimulate a change in something else, which would balance it. On the suggestion of the novelist William Golding, he called his theory the "Gaia hypothesis", after the ancient Greek name of the goddess "Mother Earth". The combination of the name and its concept of interconnectedness, made it attractive to those within the emerging New Age movement. So Gaia went beyond science into a spiritual understanding of the Earth as a living entity.

If the Eastern spiritualities were flourishing within the green movement, Christians were not absent from the cause. There were, in fact, many Christians involved with environmental concerns, and in the 1970s they began to make the connection between their love for the natural world and the positive teaching about it that could be found within the Christian faith.

The late 20th century and beyond

In the UK the growth of the Christian environmental movement came alongside a growth in Christian concern for the poor, especially in the developing world. This was not a new emphasis, and in the 19th century Christians were very much engaged in social action projects under the leadership of men such as Shaftesbury and Wilberforce. However, as secularism increased in the 20th century, some conservative Christians became more cautious of a "social gospel", believing that they should focus on salvation and personal faith. Furthermore, there were misgivings about the environmental movement because of its association with the rapidly growing New Age movement. Would involvement in environmental issues open the floodgates to pagan beliefs and practices? The earliest groups committed to the environment were therefore those coming from the more liberal, social wing of the church.

One of the first groups to be involved was the Simple Lifestyle Movement. This had the slogan "Live simply that all may simply live".[26] In 1981, the group Christian Ecology Link was formed by Christians within the secular environmental movement.[27] Christians from the evangelical end of the church began to rediscover the social dimension of the

Christian gospel around the late 1970s. One of the key books was Ron Sider's *Rich Christians in an Age of Hunger,*[28] which spoke into the consciences of many Christians of this generation.[29] In the early 1980s, television images of the Ethiopia famine had a major impact on the British public. Many Christians began to support The Evangelical Alliance Relief Fund, or "Tearfund".[30] This grew exponentially during the decade and brought social care firmly back onto the mission agenda of the evangelical churches. A concern for the environment was less visible at this time.

There were, however, signs that this too would become a significant issue. The Christian conservation organization A Rocha[31] was founded in 1983.[32] In 1997, the John Ray Initiative (JRI)[33] was founded by Sir John Houghton as a scientific think tank for the Christian environmental movement. This has contributed conferences, publications and a network of concerned scientists. It has been particularly involved in raising awareness of the issue of climate change.[34] In the United States the Au Sable Institute was founded in 1980 by Cal DeWitt, an environmental science professor. It has run courses and conferences that have brought together scientists, theologians and other specialists to further the Christian understanding of the environment.[35]

A Christian role in "Cherishing the Earth"

In our book so far we have set out the wonderful nature of our world and the serious environmental situation that we are in. We have looked at the teaching on stewardship that is common to both Judaism and Christianity, and examined the environmental implications of the fall of creation. In this chapter we have used examples to sketch out the history of Christian involvement with the environment, and how our faith has been interwoven with the development of science. We have also looked at how Christians have begun to change in their approach to the environment. Having laid these foundations, in the second half of the book we will investigate what role Christians can have in caring for God's Earth. Our practical responses are very much an outworking of our faith, and we will have a biblical focus for each chapter to continue to develop our spiritual thinking as we work out the practical implications of "Cherishing the Earth".

Individuals *can* make a difference

Gucci sandals; diamond studded wellies; Harry Potter anything, and there are still 10 presents to go – plus food; booze; cards; glad rags; CDs and DVDs. The festive season is a retail Olympics. We spend a ridiculous 15 hours hunting for the perfect gift and two hours queuing. This year, as always, Christmas is a time of Great Exhortations to spend, spend, spend.[1]

Yvonne Roberts, *The Observer*

My first trip to Bethlehem came when I was 17. I (Margot) was on a fairly intrepid school trip and Jerusalem and Bethlehem were the highlights. Coming from a Western background, I had found the traditional churches of Jerusalem difficult to connect with, but there was something different about Bethlehem. Beneath the Church of the Nativity is a cave that was used as a stable in the first century, and this is the traditional birthplace of Christ. Whether it is the "real" stable or not is a modern question. For me, as I walked down into the cave, I left behind the bustling town above and for a moment seemed to step into the first century. Here in the depths of the earth, I could focus on the miracle of the birth of Christ. It was a special moment, and one that helped to lead me towards a committed adult faith. At the time, I had just joined our local nature conservation corps and was planning an environmental career. The connection between my passion for the environment and my faith was strong at an intuitive level because I believed that nature was expressing something of God's character, and I often felt the presence of God in places of natural beauty.

However, at 17 I was not a theologian, and the environmental implications of the stable in Bethlehem would have been a mystery to me. Yet the Christian belief in the incarnation is arguably the most environmental doctrine of any faith. The birth of Christ proves God's concern for his material world and it fundamentally cuts against the belief that sees this world as something evil to be escaped from. If this were the case, Jesus could not have been born. If our material world is fundamentally evil, Jesus could not and would not have become a part of it.

This "earthed" understanding of Christ's birth is most fully explained in the first chapter of John's Gospel. John began his Gospel by deliberately echoing the start of Genesis, and this would not have been lost on his first readers. He goes back a stage from Genesis to show that, before the creation of the world, the Word (Jesus) existed. He was with God and he was God (John 1:1–2). Therefore Jesus is divine and stands outside creation. John describes him as the agent of creation and the one who gave life to humanity. Here we see the dualism between light and darkness but not between material and spiritual. This reaches a climax in the birth of Christ. He who was outside creation became a part of what he had made.

The incarnation is the greatest possible affirmation of this world and could stand on its own as sure proof of God's love for this planet. Yet it was not one static moment to prove a point. It was part of a plan of redemption that stretches back to the fall of humanity in Genesis and the

subsequent fall of creation, and looks forward to redemption through Christ's death and resurrection, and onward
to his Second Coming and the culmination of all things. A
little further on in his Gospel, John states that God so loved
the world that he gave his only son (John 3:16). The Greek
word for "world" is "cosmos". This could mean the whole of
humanity, though there are other words that more specifically mean this. Its literal meaning is the universe, which
is the whole of God's creation. The verse continues: "that
whosoever believes in him shall not perish but have eternal
life. For God did not send his Son into the world to con-
demn the world but to save the world through him" (John
3:17). From this we can conclude that our salvation as
Christians is an individual thing and we receive eternal life
individually through faith. God's mission is for his whole
world, however, and our faith as individuals equips us for
working out God's plan for the world. God's plan of salvation is for the whole cosmos, and we work towards the
time when our universe will be redeemed and renewed (see
Chapter 11). Our task now is to be a practical part of that
renewing and a life-giving sign of hope in a world that
seems far from redemption.

So in this chapter we are going to investigate very practical issues and ask how we as individuals can make our
faith work out in very down to earth ways.

If we want to make a difference as individuals to the
well being of God's creation there are a whole variety of
things we can do. Of course an individual might decide to
join with others to do this, and we will look at this shortly.
For now we need to consider the effects of our individual
lifestyles on the planet. The key areas we will look at are
housing, transport, food, consumerism and waste. At least
with regard to climate change, housing and transport are
the biggest direct sources of carbon emissions for

individuals, and food is one of the big indirect sources.[2] However, it is important to remember that climate change is not the only environmental problem, and individuals can make important contributions to solving the world's other problems.

Housing

The direct carbon emissions of the typical British individual are 6.0 tonnes per annum, of which 2.3 are attributed to housing.[3] In other parts of the developed world the figures will be different, but obviously housing is a key source of carbon emissions, and this is something that we can all tackle. In temperate climates such as the UK about half the emissions are due to heating, but in warmer climates, such as parts of the United States, air conditioning may dominate household energy use. In cooler countries we can cut emissions either by using less power, or by taking measures to decrease heat loss. A more efficient boiler would reduce energy use, whereas measures such as cavity wall insulation, loft insulation, and double glazing reduce heat loss. It is also possible to generate additional power using solar panels or wind turbines, and small household units are slowly becoming available, but these are more costly measures. Inside the house there are many other smaller energy saving ideas, including low energy light bulbs, more efficient appliances, and simply remembering to switch off power on appliances. Some people will want to take this further, and one person did just that. Averil Stedeford is a retired psychiatrist who worked for many years in a hospice, and is a member of St Columba's United Reformed Church in Oxford. She tells us how she responded as an individual.

The Greenest Semi – Averil Stedeford

Three years ago my husband died, leaving me in our lovely home which was really too big for one, and not very suitable for growing old. We cared a lot about the environment and were among the first to buy a hybrid (petrol-electric) car. Soon I felt myself nudged to sell up and buy an ordinary house near shops and buses, and to use the spare money to make it as green as possible (see photo 13). I found an architect specializing in the environment and together we planned. We chose very efficient timber framed double glazing from Denmark (see photo 14). A draughtproof porch was added. The existing kitchen was tiny so we put a timber framed extension across the back of the house, insulated with fleece, cedar clad with cedar shingles on its roof. We included a downstairs toilet with a shower large enough to accommodate a chair. Solar panels on the roof supply hot water and also the underfloor heating in the extension. The boiler was moved into the loft. A tank buried in the garden collects the rain from the roof to flush toilets, wash clothes, and serve an outside tap (see photo 15). Cavity-wall and loft insulation, organic paint and low energy light bulbs complete the project. The house is now lovely as well as efficient. The local press gave publicity. Sage, a Christian environmental group, set up a website.[4] *The Observer* gave it an Ethical Award, which led to TV coverage.

Groups of people now come to visit and learn. Some of the workmen were sceptical but now there is a team of groundsmen, carpenters, plumbers, electricians, decorators, etc. who all understand environmental concerns and have new skills. All I did was take the opportunity life gave me. Perhaps my new home should be called "Mustard Seed House".

Transport

The transport you use will depend very much on where you live, and how much you need to travel. As we live in Oxford, it is relatively easy for us to get around by walking or on buses. Many people cycle in Oxford, and driving a car is strongly discouraged by the real difficulties of finding anywhere to park. For much of the time we could do without a car. However, if we were living in a more rural location in the UK, a car would be essential for our modern working lifestyle, and we might even need two. If we wish to decrease our carbon emissions then walking or cycling is preferable to public transport, which is a much better option than using the car. On the whole it is better to keep a car going as long as possible rather than getting a new one, as considerable amounts of energy are used to make a car.[5] When the car finally comes to the end of its life the energy efficiency of the new car is an important feature to consider.

Undoubtedly, flying is coming under pressure. For many people in Europe and the United States the easiest way to cut carbon emissions is to reduce or even stop flying.[6] In 2006 the Bishop of London, Richard Chartres, even went so far as to state that flying on holiday is a "symptom of sin". This caused a considerable uproar. One snag with an abrupt decrease in flights is that it would cause harm to the economies of many countries, some of which rely heavily on tourism. Reducing the numbers of unnecessary flights, such as those to France when we have a very convenient train via the Channel Tunnel, is definitely a good thing. In all probability the era of the cheap flight will be very short as Peak Oil bites and fuel prices rocket. It is also likely that governments will bring in either carbon taxes or some type of personal carbon credit scheme, which will almost certainly reduce the number of flights in the near future. We will look at these options in Chapter 8.

Food

Another area in which the individual can make what appear to be very obvious choices in favour of environmental living is in food purchasing. In recent years, Christian Ecology Link[7] has promoted the LOAF principle:

L= locally produced

O= organically grown

A= animal friendly

F= fairly traded.

All of the above can have direct or indirect environmental benefits, and we will look at each in turn.

Locally produced

Last New Year we were staying in a cottage in Odcombe, a Somerset village. On walking through the village we spotted some bags of leeks hanging on a post that were for sale: just put 60 pence through a nearby letterbox and take them! Evidently this must have come from someone with an overabundance of leeks from their garden. We got a bag, and brought them back to our cottage to cook that evening. Minimal food miles and carbon emitted!

In a world where we must be aiming at reducing our carbon emissions, it makes sense to look at how far our food has been transported and by what means. It has been estimated that, in the UK, the food supply chain is responsible for around 20% of our carbon emissions.[8] There are some interesting statistics on the environmental costs of transporting food in from abroad. For instance, for every 1 kg of blueberries imported by plane from New Zealand to the UK, 10 kg of carbon dioxide are emitted. Even food grown in a particular country may well have been moved around the country several times en route from the farm to the supermarket shelf. So the best way of cutting down on food miles is to buy direct from farm shops, get a locally produced vegetable box, or buy from a farmers' market. In the UK farmers' markets have shown an astonishing growth: in 1997 there were none, but by 2007 there were 600, which accounted for sales of £2 billion.[9]

However, the growth in "local" is not without its critics. According to *The Economist*, trucking tomatoes from Spain to the UK in the winter may be better for the environment than growing tomatoes in a heated British greenhouse.[10] Of course, if we change to buying seasonal produce then this problem vanishes. It also appears that in Britain over half of the food-vehicle miles (number of miles travelled by vehicles carrying food) are travelled by cars visiting shops. Although these journeys are usually short they are frequent, and millions happen every day. *The Economist* is sceptical on the issue of local food, and feels that supermarkets, with their efficient centralized distribution chains and packed lorries, have considerable advantages. However, one factor that they did not mention was that fuel prices are likely to increase in the near future as governments bring in carbon taxes. It is certainly going to become less and less economic to transport food long distances. So buying local produce looks a good option for the future, and it is probably a good idea to develop the infrastructure for delivering the "local" option sooner rather than later.

Organically grown

Organic agriculture is not a new phenomenon. Of course, until the Industrial Revolution all crops were organic. It was only with the development of inorganic fertilizers and pesticides that "conventional" agriculture as we know it came into being. Organic agriculture basically involves growing crops and producing livestock in the almost complete absence of artificial chemicals. It is regulated and certified organic by one of the certification bodies, and there are ten such bodies in the UK, with many more around the world.[11] Organic food is now big business, and in 2003 the UK sales exceeded one billion pounds for the first time. Only the United States and Germany have bigger organic markets. There are two main reasons why people buy organic produce. Firstly, there are many who believe that organic is better nutritionally, and has fewer chemical hazards. Secondly, there are those who believe that it is better for the environment.

Once I (Martin) was demonstrating in an undergraduate practical class that involved caterpillars eating cabbage. Our technical staff normally bought organic cabbages, as there was a slight concern that pesticide residues on the cabbage might affect the results of the experiments. That time, though, the technicians could find only a few organic cabbages, and had to supplement the caterpillars' diet with conventionally grown cabbage. The results of this accidental experiment were very unexpected. The caterpillars munched their way happily through the organic cabbage, but keeled over and rapidly died just from walking on the conventional cabbage. It was a dramatic demonstration that there really are pesticide residues on food. Of course the pesticide used will have been aimed specifically at insects, and the amount needed to kill a small insect is much less than that needed to damage a human. Even so, our students learnt that carefully washing vegetables is definitely a good idea!

There is considerable debate about whether organic food is safer or more nutritious to eat. On one side of the argument are government departments such as the Food

Standards Agency[12] in the UK, which feels the evidence is simply not available to suggest that organic is better than conventionally grown food. On the other hand, the organic lobby, headed by the Soil Association, has no doubts: "Put simply, organic food contains more of the good stuff we need – like vitamins and minerals – and less of the bad stuff that we don't – pesticides, additives and drugs."[13] Those in favour of conventional agriculture point out that organic produce has a greater chance of infestation by potentially pathogenic microbes and fungi, as was undoubtedly the case in the past. In this often heated argument both sides can dismiss the other, with the result that it is very difficult to be sure who is correct.

The environmental issues surrounding organic agriculture are almost as contentious. As no inorganic fertilizers are used, it avoids the pollution problems of conventional agriculture (particularly nitrate and phosphate run off). However, organic fertilizers such as manure and slurry can also be polluting if they run off into waterways. Inorganic fertilizers (particularly nitrogenous fertilizers) use a lot of energy in their manufacture, adding considerably to carbon emissions.[14] In the future, as fuel prices increase, we would expect the cost of such fertilizers to increase markedly. The addition of organic residues to soil improves soil quality, and helps prevent soil erosion. Crops grown under organic regimes produce lower yields when compared to conventional agriculture. This means that organic produce is generally more expensive to produce and buy. Critics also suggest that organic agriculture cannot feed the world population, and will use more land. In some cases organic agriculture is more intensive than conventional agriculture, and less good for biodiversity. Finally, organic is not necessarily the most environmentally friendly option, particularly when it is transported long distances. In the UK, 56% of organic produce is imported.

Organic can be seen as a fad that only the well-off in Western countries can afford, and not a sensible way to produce food. However, one year we visited the Asian Rural Institute (ARI) in Japan,[15] and they certainly turn those ideas on their head. ARI trains rural development workers and pastors in the techniques of organic and sustainable agriculture. Their idea is that organic agriculture is valid in the developing world where Western agricultural models often do not apply. In many developing countries farmers simply cannot afford expensive fertilizers and pesticides. What they do have is large amounts of relatively cheap labour to keep the weeds and pests under control. So if the best techniques for organic or low-input agriculture can be developed and applied, then it could be a real advantage to the developing world farmers, and they would also gain a measure of independence from the large multinational agrichemical companies.

Animal friendly
There is little doubt that becoming a vegetarian or a vegan has potential benefits for the environment. It requires much more energy to produce meat than it does vegetables. However, humans are omnivores and eat both meat and vegetables, and there is very little sign that vegetarianism is likely to dominate, at least in Western cultures. So Christian Ecology Link, among others, has promoted the concept of "animal friendly". Although how we care for animals has little direct environmental impact, it is surely correct and a moral duty that we should look after our animals in the best way possible. If animals are to be slaughtered, it should be done in as humane a way as possible.

However, it is not always totally clear what is most animal friendly. We once visited a farm where we saw a large chicken house placed in a wood. The idea was that the chickens would wander around the wood, and come back to their house to roost – "free range". However, most of the chickens actually preferred staying permanently inside! On another occasion a battery hen farmer almost persuaded us that his hens were better looked after than free range hens. Maybe this is not as simple as it looks either.

Fairly traded

The Fair Trade movement has shown phenomenal growth. The Fair Trade mark was launched in the UK in 1994, and by 2004 sales in that country were over £100 million. Now 20 countries make up an international movement. Fair Trade focuses on social and economic justice, and aims to pay producers in the developing world a fair price for their produce. In volatile international markets, Fair Trade companies set guaranteed bottom prices, below which they will not drop. This enables the producers to plan ahead, sure that a certain level of income will be coming in. Fair Trade producers are democratic, employ no child labour, and are often environmentally friendly. The companies aim to link the farmer to the shareholder and the consumer, frequently providing stories of how Fair Trade has benefited a local community in a developing country.

Fairly traded produce is now of good quality, but there is still only a relatively limited range of products available. Critics of Fair Trade correctly point out that only co-operatives can participate at present, and that this disadvantages other local farmers. In theory it might keep world market prices artificially high, but this would really be a serious prospect only if it grew to take a much larger section of the market. There is no doubt that fairly traded products are generally more expensive, but this reflects the real cost of production. It is easy to criticize Fair Trade, but until world trade is considerably reformed in favour of developing countries it is one of the few reliable ways of redressing the trade imbalance (for more on trade with developing countries, see Chapter 9).

What can we do?
It is very evident from the above that it is not that easy being an ethical environmental consumer. What seem like simple black and white choices are much more complex. Then, if like us, you have a hectic life, you will probably not have the time to research every item you buy. Everyone will be different, and much will depend on where you live, the size of your family, your level of income, and so on, but what do *we* do?

We live in a first floor flat in Oxford. Margot mostly walks to work, while I walk a short distance to catch a bus. In both cases we walk past some local shops. So on the way back from work we both often pick up groceries from these shops and the local market. It is more expensive to use local shops, but it means less use of the car, and a significant saving on time as we make fewer dedicated shopping trips. We also want to support our local community; we like our local shopkeepers, and if we do not use our local shops we will lose them. When we need a larger shopping trip we mostly go to the Co-op as they have very good ethical policies, and we try to combine shopping using the car with a trip for another purpose.

Once actually inside a shop we tend to look out for LOAF articles, but we are not purist about this. So most of the tea and coffee we buy is fairly traded, but if it is not available at a particular shop we would rather buy non-Fair Trade than make an extra car journey. We refuse to buy apples from the southern hemisphere, and wait for European apples to arrive (particularly British!). We eat vegetarian food quite often because we enjoy it, and by buying meat less often we can afford better quality that is free range or organic. We take every opportunity to buy local products, and for many years used to get an organic vegetable box every week from a local farm. At present we do not get a box as it does not fit with our life in Oxford, but will no doubt return to vegetable boxes in the future. So this is what we do, and it is not perfect, but we are trying!

Conclusion on food

Taking action at an individual level is not that easy. Almost every action, when you look at it closely, has both positive and negative effects. Summing up an otherwise highly sceptical leader article in *The Economist* the writer says, "The best thing about the spread of the ethical-food movement is that it offers grounds for hope. It sends a signal that there is an enormous appetite for change and widespread frustration that governments are not doing enough to preserve the environment, reform world trade or encourage development. Which suggests that, if politicians put these options on the political menu, people might support them."[16] This statement could just as easily be applied to other areas such as housing, energy and transport. So be comforted: even if we make the "wrong" ethical choice by accident, but are seen by politicians and others with power to be trying to get it right, then it is worth it. They might just take notice and bring in some sensible legislation on world trade and environment. The idea that governments may pay heed is not as far-fetched as it might seem, and the Gleneagles G8 meeting of 2005 stated in their Africa communiqué that they "welcome the growing market for fair-trade goods and their positive effect in supporting livelihoods and increasing public awareness of the positive role of trade in development".[17]

Reduce, Reuse, Recycle

When I (Margot) was fourteen, my sister, Dena, gave me a fountain pen for my birthday. She had just started work and it was a generous present. I used my pen for all my school and university exams but somewhere along the way it fell into disuse. I've been feeling unhappy about using disposable pens, casting them into landfill each time, and this year repaired my fountain pen and brought it back into use. It is not only more sustainable, but writes beautifully and is a lovely connection to family. Reusing is far better than disposing of things, and reducing and recycling all play their part in the battle against domestic waste.

Back in the early 1990s in Oxford we were encouraging churches to get involved in recycling schemes. Then the council improved its own provision with bottle banks and better recycling facilities. In the last year this has gone one step further, with kerbside collection of recycling. The scheme is quite complex, with different coloured boxes for a whole array of items. It takes quite a while each week to sort everything into the boxes. Oxford is currently recycling 19% of its waste, and it is hoping to increase that to over 40% in the near future. The church recycling schemes are no longer needed, at least in their original form, as their functions have been taken over by local government. This picture is being repeated across the UK, and throughout the developed world.

The reasons for this increased interest in recycling are complex, but a major one is simply that we are running out of large holes in which to deposit waste. In the UK, 100 million tonnes of waste goes into 12,000 landfill sites every year. Despite the considerable emphasis now being placed on recycling, this is only one part of the waste equation. Waste management experts would prefer us to consider how we might reduce the amount of waste we produce. Packaging, in particular, is a major problem in this respect, and is one that is only just beginning to be addressed. To tackle all these problems, Jon Hale, an Anglican vicar and waste management specialist, has created a resource for the church about waste reduction, reuse and recycling entitled "Stewarding the Earth's Resources".[18]

How can we decrease the amount of goods going into landfill? One possibility is to use a group like Freecycle,[19] where you can offer your unwanted goods for collection by someone who wants them. So this would be the "Reuse" part of the equation. Reducing rubbish at source is even better. We were given two very strong black cotton bags by Magnus Wåhlin, the environmental secretary of Växjö diocese[20] in Sweden, when he visited us once, and we have used them many times since instead of plastic bags. We travel around many church halls giving talks on the environment, and there are still many places using disposable or plastic cups, plates and cutlery. They don't even hide them when they know we are coming! A final R many people would like to see added to the list is "Refuse". In other words, try to make conscious decisions to buy products with as little packaging as possible. So remembering your three or even your four Rs will go some way towards protecting God's creation.

Responding to consumerism

From fast food to disposable cameras and from Mexico to South Africa, a good deal of the world is now entering the consumer society at a mind-numbing pace. By one calculation, there are now more than 1.7 billion members of "the consumer class" today – nearly half of them in the "developing" world. A lifestyle and culture that became common in Europe, North America, Japan, and a few other pockets of the world in the twentieth century is going global in the twenty-first.[21]

In the developed world we are all under considerable pressure to spend money. We are even under pressure to buy on credit when we do not have the money. Children are under pressure to buy every time they switch on the television. Jonathon Porritt, chairman of the UK Sustainable Development Commission, believes that consumerism is one of the biggest problems facing the planet.[22] He has often stated that two additional planets would be needed if the whole world population consumed at the same level as in the UK. Porritt is surely correct that changing to "ethical" shopping is not going to be enough; we need to shop less than we do. The whole of this chapter has been about making choices in our lifestyle. The Bible has much to say on how we should live our lives, and we will now complete our brief survey of individual responses to the environmental crisis by considering some passages from Matthew's Gospel.

Jesus' teaching on lifestyle

The Sermon on the Mount in Matthew's Gospel gives significant teaching for those interested in living more simply. In the Beatitudes (Matthew 5:1–12), Jesus challenges a culture that values people because of the power they hold or the possessions they own. Those who are blessed are not the rich or the powerful or the strong, but the poor, the meek, the merciful and the peacemakers. If we follow Jesus' teaching we should love our enemies (5:43–48), give to the needy (6:1–4) and not store up treasure on Earth (6:19–24). The language is uncompromising. We cannot serve two masters, and so we must choose between serving God and going after materialism. If we fail to do this, we will find our eyes will be dim.

In other words, the way to keep a clear sight of our faith and of the purposes of our life is not to become too cluttered with the goods of this world. This might sound anti-material and therefore seem to be viewing the material world in a negative way. To clarify his point, Jesus continues with his famous passage about the lilies of the field (6:25–34). He instructs his disciples not to worry about what they will eat or what they will wear. He uses the examples of the birds of the field that are fed by our heavenly Father, and the lilies of the field that are clothed more finely than King Solomon. The message from Christ is clear. Living simply does not mean despising this world, it means appreciating it more fully and adjusting our lifestyle so we can be more focused on the really important things of this life.

Buried within the Sermon on the Mount is Jesus' teaching on salt and light (Matthew 5:13–16). Jesus, in teaching us how to live, commands us to be salt for those around us, giving flavour to our communities. His followers must be light so that others "may see your good deeds and praise your Father in Heaven".

Living out Jesus' teaching today

How can we live out the Beatitudes in the 21st century? If we look at the lifestyles of Jesus and his disciples in the Gospels as a whole, we find that they are significantly "downsized" from those of the people around them. The same would be true of the members of the early church. They were encouraged not to seek after material gain and to share with one another. As the environmental problems of this century become "real" for people in all parts of the world, people in the West will be forced to downsize their lifestyles, partly because the cost of energy is going to continue to rise at a rate well above our rise in incomes. If Christians have themselves downsized their lifestyles they will be in a position to provide help to those around them, who may not downsize until they are forced to.[23] This is a very practical way in which we can be salt and light to the communities in which we live, and prepare to be a substantial ray of hope to the people around us, when life in the 21st century will begin to get tough. To do this successfully, we will need to work at community level and this will be the focus of the next chapter.

7

Caring as communities

What we're seeing is a new social movement, whose significance we haven't yet fully understood. It's one of the most fascinating developments of our time. What's happening is that people who wrote off faith years ago are now being somewhat startled to discover that some of the most influential ideas and projects are now coming out of the faith communities.[1]

Rt Hon Stephen Timms MP

St Colman and corncrakes

One of the most gorgeous islands we know is Inishbofin, off the coast of Connemara in Ireland (see photo 16). Admittedly, we visited it on a startlingly beautiful summer day. Arriving by boat across the short stretch of sea separating it from the mainland, we walked towards the eastern part of the island where the beaches stretched out in pure white into an almost turquoise sea. In the distance the hills of Connemara rose out of the haze, providing a beautiful and mystical backdrop to the scene. In the southeast corner of the island there is the ruin of a 14th century chapel, itself built on the ruins of a much earlier chapel. In 664, St Colman of Lindisfarne came here to set up a monastic community, which flourished for several centuries in this remote part of the British Isles. St Colman went into exile after the Synod of Whitby refused to allow Celtic Christians to celebrate Easter by their traditional calendar.[2] Colman had defended the tradition of the local Christians in Britain but was defeated by an eloquent young monk who wished to modernize the Celtic church and bring it under Roman rule. St Colman gathered his monks from Lindisfarne and travelled westwards, via Iona, in search of a spot to live in community beyond the centralizing influences of the church.

Today, the site of Colman's monastery on Inishbofin is home to others forced off the mainland by modernizing practices. Corncrakes (*Crex crex*) are increasingly rare birds because of modern farming methods. These ruins are also the local cemetery, but when local residents found the corncrakes, they resolved not to cut the grass during the breeding season, to enable them to nest there. Amid the graves and the stinging nettles the corncrakes nest in peace. I am sure St Colman would be happy to find another community enjoying his haven from modernity.

Jesus and community

If we want to understand community and how we can and should be involved, we can find no better example than the life of Jesus. Jesus was born into a traditional community that had a strong concept of extended family and collective identity as "belonging together". This comes across most clearly in Luke, which even starts with a story about the birth of Jesus' cousin, John, and goes into detail about a visit between the two mothers. When Jesus was twelve he was left behind in Jerusalem precisely because his parents assumed he was with their relatives and friends. The group was so secure that parents did not specifically look out for their own offspring. Throughout his life, Jesus was involved in the community festivals of his faith and

travelled to Jerusalem for Passover in the spring and
Tabernacles at the end of harvest.[3] He took an active part
in his local synagogue and preached regularly. He worked
as a local carpenter and this took him into people's homes
and workplaces. It would have made him very aware of the
work they did as he designed tools and other objects for
them to use.

His view of community, however, was wider than his
own village and surrounds. His reason for coming into
conflict with his own community was his insistence that
God's blessing was for Gentiles as well as Jews. This challenged the accepted community boundaries, which could
not be widened without significant change. During the
three years of his full-time ministry, he built a community
of disciples around him and also taught and related to a
much wider community of people, both Jewish and
Gentile. Most of Jesus' miraculous healings were not of his
own disciples but of those outside his own circle. For
example, in Luke 7:1–10 there is the story of Jesus healing
the servant of a Roman centurion. Jesus gave value to
every person, whether they were male or female, slave or
free, Jewish and of his own people, or Gentile and therefore of another race. A central part of his teaching was to
"love your neighbour as yourself". When he was asked to
explain this commandment, he told the famous story of the
Good Samaritan (Luke 10:25–37).

So the whole ethos of the way Jesus lived was to build
a community of disciples who would have a close community life of their own but also be an integral part of the
wider community around them. If we move on in the New
Testament to look at the very early church, we find this
same pattern. In Acts 2:42–47 we have a description of the
closeness of the first Christians, who held everything in
common. Yet they were also a public community, meeting

daily in the Temple courts, and as a result their numbers grew. Later on, in Paul's letters, it becomes clear that the early Christians were doing a number of different jobs; there were slaves and masters among them and there were women. The descriptions are intensely collective: only a few letters were to individuals and these were to give instructions about the leadership of the Christian communities.[4]

Contrasting communities

In Europe and America our increased wealth has often led to a more privatized lifestyle. We drive to be with people of similar interests, rather than walk and interact with those immediately around us. We protect our property, but in doing so we keep others out of our lives. Children generally grow up in a much safer environment than previous generations but they too can find themselves more isolated. Jamie Carr spent part of his childhood in Uganda and now lives in the UK. His story compares the very different lifestyles in these countries and their impact on the quality of local community life for a teenager.

Growing up in Uganda: Jamie Carr

In the four years between 1996 and 2000 I had the privilege of living in Uganda: I was eleven when we went and fifteen when we came back. From the experience I have had I can see many differences in the way people live and grow up (I won't say work because I was too young) over there and back in England. The most important issue is probably the degree of responsibility and independence children have. In England it is often common for adults to want to know where children in their care are, to protect or care for them, and this can go on up to the age of 16–17. I definitely have friends who are checked up on by their parents at the age of 17. In Uganda this idea is absurd. Children as young as six or seven are caring for siblings and carrying water, and not only is this common, it's expected. There is also the issue of what children do in their spare time. In England a child will commonly "go home" after school. Then they will probably stay inside watching TV or playing on the computer, sometimes with one or two friends. In Uganda my brother and I (he is two and a half years younger) were very rarely "indoors" at all and we spent a large amount of time away from home in the company of up to 20 assorted friends, the local crowd of boys (the girls did more work and were usually busy). This group all lived close by and we saw each other every day.

One last major difference that I would like to mention is the lack of any restrictions on what we could do. An adult would threaten a beating or similar but they would have to catch us first. Climbing on the roof of the Bishop's kitchen and stealing his mangoes was risky but fun, often ending in a mad dash away while trying to look innocent. There was no tradition of being told not to do something because it was dangerous; we just did it and got hurt, sometimes badly. I feel that, having experienced both, I prefer to make my own decisions and to be constantly in the company of friends than to be in some ways isolated and protected.

The local church

For many people in modern cities, our communities are not so much the place where we live as the people we choose to mix with, and this also applies to Christian communities. In Oxford, as in many cities today, Christians have a very wide range of churches from which to choose. If you are an Anglican there are Anglo-Catholic, Liberal Catholic, Charismatic Evangelical, Reformed Evangelical, and quite a number that defy categories! Then there are Baptists, Methodists, Pentecostals, United Reformed Churches, house churches, Catholics, and Orthodox. Like our supermarket shelves, there is just so much choice. What inevitably happens is that Christians tend to choose the flavour of church that suits them best. Even among the Anglicans, only a relatively small proportion of people actually go to their own parish church. So congregations tend to be made up of like-minded people rather than Christians who live near their church. Some people are willing to drive fifteen or more miles to church on a Sunday. Of course, there is usually less public transport available on Sunday. Perhaps it is not too surprising that a thesis Martin once read showed that Christians drive more on a Sunday than during the week.

The situation in the British countryside is in marked contrast to that in the cities. Quite often the church is the one institution left in the village, after pubs, post offices, shops and schools have all closed. Very largely, but not entirely, Anglican churches are the only ones remaining in the rural villages, and the other denominations are mostly urban. So Christians living in villages have the choice of going to their local Anglican church or a long commute to a nearby town. As a result, people with vastly different theological standpoints find themselves pitchforked into the same church. Somehow they have to get on with each other!

Of course there are very good missiological reasons why Christians are best attending their local church. To reach out to a local community, people really need to live in that community. Furthermore, if you believe that God has placed you in a particular geographical location, it makes sense to worship locally and be the body of Christ there. This is a practical expression of the belief that God is interested in people and the rest of creation. There are also good environmental reasons. It simply cannot be a good practice to commute a long distance to church, when there is one nearby that really needs you.

Christians and community involvement

We can conclude that the most natural way for Christians to live out their faith is to be a part of a local worshipping community. This itself is an integral part of a wider community that reaches out still further to other communities in our own country and in other lands. It is not biblical to be either a lone Christian or a Christian community in isolation; we have an obligation to be involved in the whole neighbourhood in which we live.

We might ask how we should relate to our wider communities. Alongside traditional ideas of mission, as a church fellowship embedded in a wider community we have a specific calling to live out our Christian values in a visible way.[5] Some of the most well-known and inspiring passages from Paul's letters, such as 1 Corinthians 13, Philippians 4:4–9, and Colossians 3:12–17, were written to young Christian communities to encourage them to live out a Christian life in the context of the world around them. It is easy to set up a Christian subculture and live a Christian life by withdrawing from those around you. It is far harder, but far more rewarding, to live one's life fully integrated within a local neighbourhood and involved in its concerns.

Recent research on communities in the UK has revealed the importance of churches in community regeneration.[6] In fact, a high proportion of all voluntary work in the UK is undertaken by the church or church organizations. This is also mirrored by voluntary groups from other faith communities. A number of organizations facilitate community involvement. The quote from Stephen Timms at the start of this chapter came from his speech at an awards ceremony of Faithworks, which is one of the most active organizations.[7] Founded by Steve Chalke, Faithworks seeks to enable Christian groups to undertake community projects, and is particularly helpful with projects coming out of the UK government's Strategic Partnership initiative.

None of this appears specifically "environmental". The ecological dimension begins to emerge if our values include the intrinsic worth of all of God's creation and of our responsibility to be caring stewards of the whole world around us. We will then naturally find ourselves with a strong set of environmental values, which we will start to work out in our communities. These environmental ethics will connect up with our principle of care towards humans, so that our approach will become truly holistic. In fact, as we investigate what we can do to be more environmentally friendly at local community level, we will find that living more sustainably enables and encourages greater community involvement. It is the place where the needs of people and planet can be met most wholesomely.

This commitment to community does not end with our neighbourhood. Humans and non-humans in other parts of the world are also affected by our actions, reminding us that we are a global community. The church is already global – it almost certainly has more community bases worldwide than any other organization or group. This, combined with Christian values and especially the ethos of self-giving, provides an enormous opportunity for environmental involvement worldwide, and we will consider this further in Chapters 9 and 10. If we grasp the moment, it will enrich our church lives as we find ourselves enriching the lives of those around us. This may sound idealistic but it can be worked out in very practical ways. We can start by making a survey of our own local area and use this as we seek to become more "local" in the way we live our lives. This is quite easy to do at a basic level, and you can use the survey we have provided at the end of this chapter. There are many possibilities for increasing sustainability through community involvement, and we will outline some of these in this chapter.

Growing sustainable communities: Grove

Three of our happiest years were spent in the village of Grove in South Oxfordshire (or "occupied Berkshire", as some of the locals called it). We moved there when I (Margot) became curate of the parish church and soon found ourselves very much part of a growing community in the Thames Valley area. Grove had expanded in the 1970s and 80s on land that had been a large US air base in the Second World War. There was still a memory of those days and I can remember visiting one woman who had queued with her husband as a newly married couple to "get a missen hut" (prefabricated military building) and set up home at the end of the war. There is still a considerable amount of airfield land and not surprisingly this has been earmarked for major development in the housing development plans for the Thames Valley. The development will almost double the size of the village and would need careful planning if the good community spirit were to be retained.

There are also significant environmental challenges. Our vicar, Revd John Robertson, had become the Faith Representative for the local Strategic Partnership, and the planners came to Grove to talk to the local church ministers' meeting as we, collectively, represented the largest community group. There are many practical environmental issues to address. There are plans to make the new housing stock sustainable by building eco-housing.[8] Factors as diverse as waste water and local schooling all have an environmental impact and these need to be planned to maximize sustainability. Water provision is an issue, and proposals for a new reservoir on nearby farmland are on the table amid local opposition. Perhaps the biggest issues concern employment and transport. There are no plans to increase employment in the village by developing the local business park, and instead employment is expected to be in two employment centres outside of the village. Public transport is poor and, although there are plans to design out the use of the car in the new development, there is little option for many people for their journey to work. There will inevitably be a need for new link roads to adjacent villages. Local council plans for encouraging greater use of public transport simply hope to "persuade" people to change. With independent bus and rail services, it is difficult to manage this effectively. There were plans to reopen the railway station (closed by Beeching![9]) but this would be dependent on rail companies agreeing to provide a suitable service.

One of the key roles of churches in sustainability in Grove is to run groups for different sectors of the village. Our church has everything from toddlers, through large youth clubs, to friendship groups for older people and bereavement care. All these provide services and activities in the village and prevent yet another journey outside. The church services themselves are also a part of this – especially if people walk or cycle to them! The churches in Grove jointly run a fantastic café in the village, called "Cornerstone", which also sells fairly traded goods and books.[10] It is always busy and is a great place to meet people or have lunch or just a coffee with a friend. Again, by having something in the village it prevents more journeys.

The very warm and supportive churches in Grove mean that they are well placed to play a full part in the growth of the village and to help its growth to be a sustainable one.

Transition Towns

One of the most exciting new concepts in developing sustainable communities is that of Transition Towns.[11] This has been principally motivated by fears of what will happen after Peak Oil. The idea is that a town or other size of community sets up a group to look at how they might prepare for a world without oil, and where energy supplies will be much more constrained. Many topics need to be considered, for example, transport, housing, waste and food. Where possible the idea is to co-ordinate activities that are already happening and give them a new focus. The first Transition Town in the UK was Totnes, which is working on an Energy Descent Action Plan for the town. In August 2007, fifteen towns, three cities (Bristol, Exeter and Nottingham), and three other areas, all in the UK, were actively engaged in this process. There are people looking at the idea for Oxford, but this is only at the preliminary stages.

Faith in communities

In 2004, Martin was invited to participate in an online discussion forum, "Faith and sustainable development: Mapping your practice", which was organized by the WWF-UK[12] and the Sustainable Development Commission (SDC)[13], the UK government's independent adviser on sustainable development. It was an interesting experience "meeting" people from a number of faith groups, although the dominant group were Christians. We shared our experiences of how we were attempting to "green" our communities, and found that, at least in this respect, we had a lot in common. Most of our organizations had little money, were working from back bedrooms, and felt frustrated that others in our communities did not share our vision. But one had the real feeling, even in this rather artificial environment, that there was a band of committed people out there.

Sometime later, in 2005, WWF-UK and the SDC produced a report, based partly on our online discussions, which aimed to survey UK faith communities' sustainable development activities, and to give some pointers to the next steps.[14] The executive summary of the report begins: "UK faith groups have much to offer in helping to deliver sustainable development. Rooted in their locality over generations, defined by a strong, shared set of non-materialistic values, and experienced in working together with trust and respect, faith groups are well-placed, both in outlook and practice, to influence and deliver sustainable development at all levels. Prayer and spiritual belief offer a means of support lacking in the secular world." The report is very encouraging, and includes four main case studies, one each from Muslim, Jewish, Buddhist and Christian projects. The Muslim project, Be Fikr (warm and cosy), based in Balsall Heath, a deprived area of Birmingham, aims to improve the local environment for residents. "Partners in Creation" promotes environmental awareness and action in the British Jewish community. The Buddhist case study was Windhorse Trading, which sells gifts from poorer countries in the East. St Sidwell's Centre in Exeter[15], the Christian project, focused initially on health inequalities, created a community garden and runs a café. There are many other examples of projects from across the UK cited in the report.

The one slight weakness in the survey is that almost all the projects cited are in urban locations, and it has hardly

Photo 1. View from Diomond Hill, Connemara, Ireland. Much of this area of Ireland is now covered by peat bogs, but it was once forested before humans chopped the trees down. So Connemara is beautiful but not "natural". Photo: Margot R. Hodson.

Photo 2. Ringed Plover (*Charadrius hiaticula*) on a beach near Cleggan, Connemara, Ireland. There are about 9,700 species of birds in the world, and many are under threat. Photo: Margot R. Hodson.

Photo 3. Martin Hodson and Prof. Tasuku Akagi at a Shinto shrine at the summit of Mount Fuji, Japan. Photo: Dr Naoki Kaneyasu.

Photo 4. Mount Bandai, Fukushima prefecture in central Japan, taken from Lake Inawashiro. Mount Bandai is an active volcano, and erupted in 806 and 1888. The last eruption destroyed all the surrounding villages, killing 461 people. Photo: Martin J. Hodson.

Photo 5. Spangle butterfly (*Papilio protenor*) photographed in Tokyo, Japan. Its Japanese name is Kuro-ageha, and "Kuro" means black. It is found in many countries of eastern Asia and is common in urban areas of Japan. Approximately 900,000 insect species are known to science. Photo: Margot R. Hodson.

Photo 6. Baby rabbit photographed in a deep lane between Odcombe and East Chinnock, Somerset, UK. Approximately 41,000 vertebrate species are known to science. Photo: Margot R. Hodson.

Photo 7. A temporary field pond on Otmoor, Oxfordshire, UK. The pond is notable for supporting the UK Biodiversity Action Plan (BAP) endangered aquatic plant, Tassel Stonewort (*Tolypella intricata*). In common with many temporary ponds, this one is not marked on maps, and is not visible on Google Earth. Perhaps it is not surprising that temporary ponds have been considered unimportant habitats. Photo: Jeremy Biggs (Pond Conservation).

Photo 8. Makhtesh Ramon in the Negev Desert, is 85 km south of Beersheva, Israel, and is the largest crater of its type in the world. It was formed as a result of water erosion. Now very little water falls here, and day time temperatures in the summer often exceed 40°C. Photo: Martin J. Hodson.

Photo 9. Sudbury, Ontario, Canada. Barren land caused by smelting activities and the resulting pollution. The maple in the foreground was showing one of the worst cases of dieback I (Martin) have ever seen, but amazingly was still alive! Photo: Martin J. Hodson.

Photo 10. Solling in the Black Forest, Germany, is one of the most famous sites in the world for acid rain research. The forest here has been continuously monitored since the 1970s. In this beech forest plot several different sampling devices are being used to collect rain water and leaves. The green container on the right is collecting water that has flowed down the stem of the tree. Photo: Martin J. Hodson.

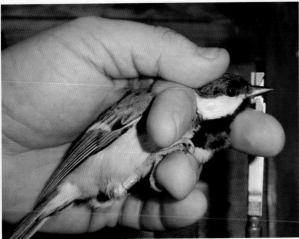

Photo 11. Great Tit (*Parus major*) being measured for bill depth. This is related to the feeding ecology of the individual, as it limits the size and types of prey that can be taken and is also correlated with the power or strength of 'bite' that can be applied. Photo: Dr. Andy Gosler.

Photo 12. Aerial photograph of the Great Plains near Winnipeg, Manitoba, central Canada, showing numerous rectangular wheat fields. Photo: Martin J. Hodson.

Photo 13. Averil Stedeford's award-winning ecohouse in Headington, Oxford, UK. The front of the house, before work began. The car is a Toyota Prius Hybrid (petrol-electric) the choice of Averil's late husband. It reflects their long term concern for the environment. Photo: Martin J. Hodson.

Photo 14. Averil Stedeford's ecohouse. Fitting of efficient timber framed double-glazing from Denmark. Photo: Martin J. Hodson.

Photo 15. Averil Stedeford's ecohouse. Building site in the back garden from above when the work to bury an underground water tank was being carried out. The hole for the water tank is protected by a wire cage, the tank is on the right, and a digger is in the foreground. The tank now collects rain from the roof to flush toilets, wash clothes, and serve an outside tap. Photo: Averil Stedeford.

Photo 16. Inishbofin, Connemara, Ireland. The ruin of a 14th century chapel, built on the ruins of an earlier chapel. In 664, St Colman of Lindisfarne came here to set up a monastic community. It is now the site of a local cemetery, and Corncrakes (*Crex crex*) breed here. Photo: Margot R. Hodson.

Photo 17. Every year in December, Sage runs a stands at the Green Fair in Oxford Town Hall. Here Caroline Steel is manning the stand which has literature, books and Fair Trade items for sale. Photo: Martin J. Hodson.

Photo 18. Ss Mary & John churchyard, on the Cowley Road in Oxford, UK. A project to restore the churchyard has won a number of awards. Photo: Martin J. Hodson.

Photo 19. St Barnabas Church, Queen Camel, nr. Yeovil, Somerset, UK. The Rector, Mike Perry (Margot Hodson's brother) leads an open air service in their churchyard. The church recognized a need within the wider community for allotment space and decided to think laterally, using the reserve churchyard plot to create the allotments. The project was joint winner of a *Church Times* National Green Church Award for "Action within the Community" in November 2007. Photo: Peter Rice.

Photo 20. Binsey Lane, Oxford, UK in July 2007. After some of the wettest June and July weather on record the River Thames burst its banks resulting in widespread flooding in Oxford. Such events are likely to increase in frequency due to climate change. Photo: Karl Wallendszus.

Photo 21. Manor Farm, Warmington, nr. Banbury, UK. John Neal explaining the history of Warmington and of his farm to a party from the Certificate in Christian Rural and Environmental Studies (CRES). Photo: Margot R. Hodson.

Photo 22. Manor Farm, Warmington, nr. Banbury, UK. John Neal leads a party around his farm showing them the environmental schemes that he has implemented. Photo: Margot R. Hodson.

Photo 23. Wind farm near Parys Mountain, Anglesey, Wales. The UK government wants 20% of energy to come from renewable sources by 2020. Photo: Martin J. Hodson.

Photo 24. Sustainable transport. Bicycles and buses outside Oxford Railway Station. Far more use of bicycles and public transport will be required in the future as we approach Peak Oil. Photo: Simon Collings.

Photo 25. Paddington Railway Station, London, UK. To reduce carbon emissions by 60% by 2050 from 1990 levels will need far greater usage of public transport. Photo: Simon Collings.

Photo 26. Boat transporting people in a flood prone area of Gopalganj District, Bangladesh. Climate change will make flooding even more likely in this area. Photo: James S. Pender.

Photo 27. Planting coconuts in the compound tree nursery of the Church of Bangladesh Social Development Programme (CBSDP) at Meherpur, Bangladesh. These are then given free to the poor people CBSDP are working with, or sold to others at a subsidised rate to plant around their homes. Other species given out include mangos and jackfruit. Photo: James S. Pender.

Photo 28. Arif is a local man who originally took a small loan from Church of Bangladesh Social Development Programme (CBSDP) in Meherpur to establish a tree nursery. He has been very successful and has leased larger and larger amounts of land for his nursery. Now he can afford to send all his children to school and is even employing others to work with him in the nursery. More trees in Meherpur District will offset the drying effect of global warming in this area by reducing winds over fields and increasing local humidity. Photo: James S. Pender.

Photo 29. Early morning light across the village of Karsha, central Zanskar, India.
Photo: J. Seb Mankelow.

Photo 30. Zanskar, India. Zanskaris collect an important percentage of winter fodder from the threshing circle. Photo: J. Seb Mankelow.

Photo 31. Margot Hodson leading a Passover in March 2005 at the A Rocha centre, Cruzinha, on the Algarve, Portugal. Photo: Martin J. Hodson.

Photo 32. The Jordan River near Kfar Blum Kibbutz in Northern Israel. It often surprises people that the Jordan is so small. Perhaps John the Evangelist had such a scene in mind when he wrote of "the River of the Water of Life" (Rev. 22:1). Photo: Martin J. Hodson.

Photo 33. The Garden Tomb, Jerusalem. The resurrection of Jesus is significant for the whole of creation. Christ offers humanity redemption and hope through his resurrection and seals a promise of renewal for the Heavens and the Earth. Photo: Martin J. Hodson

Photo 34. Sunrise over the Sea of Galilee, Israel on New Year's Day. We are confident in the hope that creation is held together in Christ and we can trust him for the future. Photo: Martin J. Hodson.

anything to say about rural contexts. This was, however, an inevitable consequence of trying to be fair to all faiths and, in the UK, Christianity is by far the dominant faith of the countryside. This report is just one indication of the increased interest in faith groups shown by both national and local government in the UK. Increasingly, in our fragmented society, government is turning to faith groups to help with all kinds of social and sustainability issues, as these groups often represent a major focus for "community". We have a long association with one of the groups featured in the WWF-UK and SDC report, Sage, Oxford's Christian Environmental Group, and we will look at this next.

Sage: A local Christian environmental group

If there was one city in the UK where Christianity and environmentalism were most likely to come together, it was Oxford. Many thriving Christian congregations, two universities with strong environmental interests, and an active Green Party all provided the background for Sage. The group formed in St Aldate's, a large evangelical Anglican church in central Oxford. The first meeting was convened at Brasenose Farm, Oxford on 3 September 1990, and seven people (including Martin) attended. At first Sage restricted its activities to St Aldate's, but it soon spread to other churches in Oxford, and then further away. Sage regards itself as a Christian witness to environmentalists and an environmental witness to Christians. Activities include practical conservation work, production of literature, services, talks and discussions, weekends and longer periods away, guided walks and prayer meetings. Every year Sage has a stall at the Green Fair in Oxford town hall (see photo 17), and since 1999 it has participated in services on Environment Sunday in a whole variety of churches. In the mid-1990s Sage members debated whether to become a national organization, to employ staff, and to apply for charitable status. Eventually they decided to remain Oxford based and to maintain an entirely voluntary status.

Sage does, however, exert some influence at a national (and even international) level through its website.[16] At present the website is one of only 101 religious sites in the UK selected by the British Library for their permanent archiving project.[17] As sites are catalogued alphabetically in the archive, Sage currently finds itself between pop singer Sandie Shaw and Rowan Williams, the Archbishop of Canterbury, in the religion section – we think they have rather different religious views!! Close links with A Rocha led Sage to become their support group in the Oxford area,[18] and Sage has members that are supporters of all of the national Christian environmental organizations that operate in the UK. Sage has also collaborated with the Oxford Diocese, provided web space for several other local projects, and helped run two major conferences in the area on climate change. Secular agencies and groups have also worked with Sage. Oxford City Council is often in contact to help publicize their energy saving schemes. Most Sage conservation work parties have taken place at Boundary Brook, a wildlife reserve in the middle of the city that is run by the Oxford Urban Wildlife Group.[19] In 2007, Sage joined with a number of secular environmental groups to form the Oxfordshire Climate Alliance, which is co-ordinating activity on climate change across the county. Sage is now recognized as a Fresh Expression of Church[20] and is a network with a strong core of activists at the centre of a much larger and diffuse community. One of the members of the network now tells her story.

Restoring a churchyard with and for its local community

Ruth Conway is a well known and respected figure in the Christian environmental movement in Oxford, the UK and beyond. At a local community level she is also the co-ordinator of her churchyard project. Here she explains the project.

Ss Mary & John Churchyard, on the Cowley Road in Oxford, was laid out in the 1870s with trees, flowers and shrubs: an attractive peaceful place where loved ones could be remembered (see photo 18). Unfortunately, 120 years later it had become a derelict, massively overgrown, no-go area. In 2000, on the initiative of a community policeman, a group of soldiers cut back the jungle, revealing the original layout and the many, often dislodged and damaged, memorials. After then closing the churchyard for burials and consulting widely in the local community, it was decided to manage the site for wildlife, but in a way that would keep sight lines throughout. Single Regeneration Budget funding helped to resurface old paths, reopen the entrances, lower the high boundary wall and install lighting. A five-year management plan provided the guidelines for a combination of clearing and planting. This in turn required consulting with experts and residents in the area, the recruiting of volunteers through many different channels, and applying for funding from a variety of sources, in order to fulfil the vision of recreating a quiet green space for all to enjoy.

Seven years on we have a wildflower Garden of Remembrance and Thanksgiving, a mini-labyrinth as the centrepiece of a "rest space" that welcomes people in from the Cowley Road, access to memorials that have artistic and historic value, a variety of habitats for wildlife, on-site interpretation boards that introduce the many visitors to both the wildlife and the local history, and an educational website that gives this information in much more detail.[21] Early on, the church registered as an Eco-Congregation so that the work in the churchyard is seen as part of the celebration of and care for God's creation. It is also the church's best outreach project, involving people in the community of different backgrounds and experience, and appreciated by many who have no connection to the church. The gratitude of people who are now able to revisit their family graves has also been very moving.

Eco-Congregation

Ruth mentioned above that her church registered for the Eco-Congregation scheme.[22] This is a national scheme in the UK that we believe is the best way available to "green" a church congregation. Notice that we say "congregation", as applied properly it is a tool to make the whole church community more sustainable, and should also spill out into the wider local community. In 2005, Martin had an opportunity to find out more about Eco-Congregation, and wrote the following short article[23] to describe the experience:

I had known about Eco-Congregation for a number of years, so I was very pleased when Jo Rathbone, Eco-Congregation Co-ordinator for England and Wales, e-mailed me in October 2005 and asked if I would like to help assess Ss Mary & John, Cowley Road, Oxford, for an award. The church had carried out an audit in 2003, and set themselves targets to further increase their green activities. Two years later, they wanted to apply for an award, having made substantial advances. My job, and that of my co-assessor, Dr Paul Robinson (Oxford City Council) was to see how far the church had progressed since they carried out their audit. After a pre-meeting with Paul, and reading all the paperwork submitted by the church, we set the assessment for 14 December 2005. This involved meeting the project leader, Ruth Conway, the vicar, Adam Romanis, the churchwardens, and several others. We had a good look around the churchyard and the church, and assessed church activity in three main areas: worship and teaching; practical things to do with buildings and land; and outreach to the local and global community. Paul and I were convinced that St Mary & St John had met the Eco-Congregation criteria, and justified getting an award. This is the first church in Oxford to gain an award, and I hope it will not be the last!

As we write in 2007, over 100 Eco-Congregation awards have been made to churches in the UK, and in March 2007 the Eco-Congregation scheme came under the management of A Rocha UK.

Churchyard allotments

Vicars tend to run in families and Margot's brother, Mike Perry, is the Rector of six parishes in Somerset. One of these, St Barnabas Queen Camel, near Yeovil, recognized the need within the wider community for allotment space. Thinking laterally, they used their reserve churchyard to create allotments, in a scheme led by Churchwarden Paul Davis (see photo 19). Soon this land that had been a rough field, became alive with cabbages and bean poles, and a focal point for local people. This was all part of a wider green strategy for the church and in 2007 St Barnabas was joint winner of a *Church Times* National Green Church Award for "Action within the Community". For the last two years the harvest festival has gone out to the allotments, sharing the worship with the gardeners.

Broken bread and wine outpoured

Sharing communion is the most profound way in which we connect with God and one another. Christians have long realized that communion sustains individuals and the life of the community. Communion uses the "fruits of the Earth". Wheat and grapes are planted, nurtured and ripened. They are then harvested, crushed and made into bread and wine. It is a collaborative act between humans working as stewards and the rest of nature providing the seed, soil, rain and sun.

The origins of communion are in the Last Supper on the night before Jesus died. Jesus used broken bread and a cup of wine as a reminder of his death and also as a fore-taste of the banquet we will one day share with him at the end of the age. Communion therefore looks back at the death of Jesus and forwards towards a time when God, people and the cosmos are in harmony. Looking at Jesus' death, these "earthy" symbols point us to the hope of redemption coming out of his suffering. Today, as we see suffering around us among both humans and the rest of creation, sharing communion helps us to connect through the cross to this amazing hope of redemption for the whole cosmos. As we shall see in Chapter 11, this future redemption is one in which we shall be finally able to take our place in creation in the way we were first created to do, and this redeemed creation will be abundantly fruitful as in Eden.

Communion is always a community act and focused on sharing. Taking communion together should make us aware of the interconnectedness of the human and non-human communities in which we live. As we think of the sacrifice of Jesus on our behalf, so communion should be a reminder of our commitment to share sacrificially with all those around us. Communion therefore takes us into the heart of God, enables us to share deeply with one another as believers and sends us out into the community around us to connect with its concerns, to be reconciled with one another and to live in harmony with all.

Community survey

This survey works best when used in a group setting. You could make it the focus of an away day or use it in a home group. You could also use it as the basis for a questionnaire to use more widely.

1. What makes up your local community? Note down all the things in it. Include everything from trees and open spaces, to shops, businesses and places of worship. You might like to make a map to show where they are.

2. What is absent that might make your community more sustainable?

3. Is there anything missing that would provide for human need or help biodiversity?

4. In what ways is your church involved in your local area both as a body and as individuals?

5. What are the opportunities for new involvement with your local community that would be environmentally friendly?

6. What resources do you have?

7. Outline a basic strategy for sustainable community involvement. You might like to change some of the things you are already doing and you may need to prioritize some of the opportunities, depending on your resources.

National leadership will inspire change

Justice in the life and conduct of the State is possible only as first it resides in the hearts and souls of the citizens.

Plato[1]

In the last two chapters we have looked at how we might respond to the environmental crisis as individuals and as local communities. Often, though, it feels like there are things that are totally or almost totally out of our control. Once we reach the national level we can vote, we can protest, but we do not seem to have much influence. It can also feel like that at national church level. In this chapter we will look at how people are responding to the changes that are going on around them in Western industrialized societies, and what leadership is being given to make the necessary changes. Obviously, we cannot cover everything in one short chapter, and we will concentrate on farming, energy and transport, and focus mostly on the UK. Margot will introduce this with a reflection from the book of Job.

Have you comprehended the vastness of the Earth?

For many people the book of Job seems disheartening, but when examined more deeply it is essentially about hope. It is the story of a righteous man who has everything taken away from him apart from his faith in God. It is a book that helps us to understand that we cannot control everything. At the beginning of the book, Job is presented as a man who had everything finely tuned. He was the most successful farmer in his region, with huge herds of livestock, and, in modern terms, a major employer. He had a successful family life and regularly made offerings to God to make sure that all these good things stayed in place. Then the tornado of disaster swept through his life, compounded by the insensitivity of his advisers. Eventually God spoke to Job out of the storm, not immediately with words of comfort, but demanding whether Job understood him or could control his creation. At the end of the book we meet a very different Job who understands the vastness of God and his creation.[2] Job realizes God is so much greater than we are, and his universe so much greater than our potential to plan and use it. Through repentance this becomes the starting point of humility that enables Job to have a real relationship with God and a true vision for life. He begins to understand the interconnectedness of humanity with creation, and of creation and creator. When he finally sees God, he is terrifying but not to be feared. He is a real God who can be related to, loved and trusted. Once Job let go of his own agenda and began to allow God to act, he found that he had hope because it was based not on success but on relationship.[3]

Today, the biggest challenge facing national leadership, whether church, government or other organizations, is the need to give leadership for change, and to do so in a way that will inspire hope. We need a fundamental shift in our thinking in the West if we are to develop lifestyles more suited to sustainable living. To be able to persevere we are going to need hope that there is a better future up ahead. We will also need national leadership in all sectors with the humility to grasp that we may not be able to control every-thing by science and technology. Like Job, however, our leadership needs to be strong enough to face the fear of this limitation, and courageous enough to be flexible in meeting a changing situation. With these thoughts in mind, we will now turn to look at British agriculture, where the story of Job has been acted out on many UK farms in the last decade.

Agriculture and the crisis in UK farming

As I (Martin) turned to write this section, British farming had been hit another hammer blow. After recent crises over BSE,[4] foot-and-mouth and avian flu, we have just had some of the wettest June and July weather on record (2007) (see photo 20). The resulting floods were worse than those in 1947. Many newspapers and politicians specu-lated on whether this was the effect of climate change, but for the householders, businesses and farmers affected, such speculation might seem rather theoretical. The farm-ers of Oxfordshire, Worcestershire, Herefordshire and Gloucestershire were hit particularly hard. Crops, which were already growing slowly, were destroyed when they should have been harvested. The National Farmers' Union vice-president, Paul Temple, said the effect on flooded farms was "phenomenal in terms of productivity", and undoubtedly the UK will experience food shortages and price increases as a result.[5]

These disasters are bad news for British farmers, but even without them the overall economic scenario for agri-culture in the UK is very poor. The income produced by agriculture has decreased in real terms by about 40% between 1973 and 2003.[6] By 1999 UK farmers were being paid less for their goods than the cost of production. For instance, in 2002 the cost of milk production was 18 to 21 pence per litre and farmers were being paid 18.5 pence per litre. The reasons for this are complex, but it appears that the large supermarkets had gained a stranglehold on the farmers, and were making huge profits. It has also been cheaper to import some commodities from other parts of Europe than to grow them in Britain. Whatever the reasons, many farmers, faced with economic ruin, have left farming. The overall trend is towards larger farms with fewer farmers, and the average age of a farmer is increasing.

The British countryside can give the impression of never changing, but that is very definitely not the case. John Neal[7] is a farmer and Methodist lay preacher from Warmington, near Banbury. Here he tells his story.

A farmer's journey

I was born a few weeks before the D-Day invasion of France in World War II. I grew up on the family farm and have worked on it all my life (see photos 21 and 22). Now I am able to take stock of the changes that have taken place on this farm during the past 60 years.

World War II created a mindset in a generation of farmers that the farmer's *raison d'être* was to produce as much food as possible from every acre of land by whatever means were available. My father's medicine chest/chemical cabinet in those days contained a fearsome array of deadly chemicals, including cyanide to kill rabbits and strychnine to kill moles. We have now realized that most of these chemicals wreak havoc with man, beast and the environment. However, in the 1940s and 1950s our farm, one of thirteen family farms in the parish, was a truly mixed farm. The farming families and agriculture-related trades formed the backbone of village life; haymaking, harvest and spud-picking were village events. The great grain-threshing machines were always in evidence during the winter months, either crawling slowly from farm to farm or at work in the rickyard with an army of workers busily bustling around them.

The 1960s and 1970s were a time of increased wealth, scientific discovery and technological advance. Much of this, driven by the EU's Common Agricultural Policy, made it possible for a ruinous Armageddon of abuse to be released within farming practice. A programme of intensive production was instigated. Farm animals were kept in cages, hedges were torn out of the landscape, ancient grass fields – turf that had nourished countless generations of cattle, sheep and horses – were destroyed in a moment by the plough. Farming for us during that period was intensive egg production in battery cages, and all the land was given to cereal cropping. Where problems were encountered the answer was new drugs and chemical sprays. As I look back those were dark days, but, at the time, for farmers, MAFF,[8] governments and consumers, *where ignorance was bliss 'twas folly to be wise*.

Thankfully, the farming pendulum was to swing back to a saner place in the 1980s. The environmental conscience of the nation was awakening. In 1988 the first voluntary set-aside scheme was made available. We were the first farm in our area to enter that scheme, an action that invited much scorn and some verbal hostility from our neighbours. In 1991 the last of the cages used for egg production were dismantled and, from that time, a new farming regime was embraced, with half of the farm placed in a 20 year, government-financed environmental scheme. The management plan and objectives of this scheme were, in the context of the 2007 environmental schemes, naïve and foolishly simple. The idea was to create and sustain a managed pattern of short mown grass strips, areas of long grasses never to be cut, some areas of bushes, some natural forestation, and to plant some two miles of new hedge. Once initiated, then let nature, free from chemical input, take its course. The result has been good; for five years little change was noticed but then, as the effect of fertilizers wore off, natural grasses, herbs and wild flowers slowly spread from the hedgerows. Now an environment has evolved that is a haven for insects, small mammals and birds. The rest of the farm is run extremely extensively. There is no fertilizer input and the only use of chemical sprays is spot-spraying with a knapsack sprayer for pernicious weeds. We now have a small flock of sheep and make small-bale hay – sold mostly for horses, but also as bedding for hamsters, feed for alpacas, etc.

What a wealth of changes in one short lifetime. As you read this you may well feel that the farm is now in a good place. But that will be for just a few short years, and no sustainable future lies before the environmentally friendly shape it now has. My children could not afford to farm even if they wanted to, and so whither to from here? The journey continues – a stable environmental paradise is as elusive as ever.

Farm Crisis Network

Not surprisingly, all the changes happening in the British countryside have caused immense amounts of stress for the farmers involved. Here Canon Glyn Evans, the Oxford Diocese Rural Officer, describes the work of one of the organizations that are seeking to help those in the rural community adapt to the changes:

Farm Crisis Network (FCN)[9] is a national organization founded in 1995. It is a Christian organization, but it exists to support people of all faiths and none. The aims of FCN are to relieve need, hardship and distress in the farming community by providing pastoral and practical support through periods of anxiety, stress and related problems. This may involve problems within the farm business and/or the farm household. As well as providing this support, FCN also aims to raise awareness of farming issues and the needs of the farming community within the churches and in wider society. Together with RABI[10] and ARC-Addington Fund,[11] FCN is part of the Farming Help Partnership of charities providing complementary forms of support to the farming community.

FCN has a national helpline[12] staffed by trained volunteers every day of the year. It has over 250 volunteers across the UK, who come largely from the farming community and related industries and from churches. County groups are supported by a local co-ordinator. Helpline volunteers refer cases to local co-ordinators, who then assign a volunteer to visit the farm and provide whatever support is appropriate, for as long as it is needed. Calls to the helpline account for about one-third of FCN's contacts, with others coming directly to FCN through local referrals by churches and other organizations and from people connected with farming. FCN provides support for those struggling to face legislative burdens, financial problems including debt and coping with change management in the fast-moving climate of farming. Loneliness, depression and relationship problems account for some of the difficulties facing those who contact FCN. Natural disasters such as foot-and-mouth disease, avian flu, tuberculosis and extreme weather conditions also bring particular times of stress and difficulties.

Conclusion

We conclude that there have been major changes in UK agriculture in recent years. In general, environmental legislation and the move towards less intensive agriculture have been beneficial. Unfortunately, the recent series of major disasters, plus a whole set of economic problems, make life very tough indeed for many in the farming community.

Joseph: Managing the effects of climate change

The biblical tale of Joseph is a climate change story. Joseph was an accurate forecaster and found himself providentially in a position to manage the implications of his climate predictions. He expected seven years of plenty followed by seven years of famine. He must have been an outstanding personality and highly intelligent to "gain the contract" to oversee Egypt's ministries for agriculture and food. He was also a brilliant administrator and an inspirational leader. Soon the whole of Egypt was storing grain, such that when the famine set in, they not only had enough for themselves, but also had some to give away to environmental refugees, such as Joseph's brothers from Canaan.

Today the world is enjoying the last few years of plenty from our oil resources. As well as our climate changing we are facing sharp increases in the cost of fuel in the future. This will affect the cost of everything we buy. With good management we can use the fuel we have now to produce other forms of energy generation, and this will enable us to adapt to the changes that are coming this century. Joseph was able to change people's thinking towards prudent planning for the future. We need to look to those who can inspire our nations to shift in our thinking and to make this wise provision. Martin will now set out some of the options for alternative energy sources and the options on transport.

Energy

Essentially there are three main energy sources: carbon-based, nuclear and renewable. It is now clear that we need to move off carbon-based sources as quickly as possible if we are to avoid dangerous climate change.[13] As we have seen, Peak Oil may well force us to change our habits in the near future anyway. In March 2007 the UK government published its Draft Climate Change Bill.[14] The main headline features of the draft bill were legally binding targets to reduce carbon dioxide emissions by 60% by 2050, with a 26 to 32% reduction by 2020. These figures have caused a great deal of discussion, with the Stop Climate Chaos[15] coalition calling for cuts of 80% by 2050 and a minimum reduction of 30% by 2020. Others are demanding even greater emissions cuts. As many have pointed out, it is fine having targets, but how do we keep to them? Of course we can improve the efficiency of cars, decrease heat loss from buildings, and aim to lower emissions in these and similar ways. Unfortunately, although these measures will help, most authorities do not consider that energy conservation alone will be enough. The other option is to use alternative energy sources, and we will look at these next.

Renewables

At present, renewable energy sources account for about 10% of the world's energy supply. The UK government in its Energy White Paper of 2007[16] states that, as part of its strategy to combat climate change, it is setting a target such that 10% of electricity supplies shall come from renewable sources by 2010, and that this should double by 2020. In 2006, that figure was only about 4% in the UK. What are "renewables"? They are a mixed bag of technologies, including solar, wind, hydro, wave and geothermal, which have the potential to provide energy that will in principle never run out (see photo 23). They also, at least during the operational phase, do not produce carbon emissions.

The Severn Barrage

In 2006 we were contacted by John Bimson, the Old Testament tutor at Trinity College, Bristol, to ask if we could help organize a conference to look at the practical and scientific issues surrounding the Severn Barrage proposal, and then to assess it from the perspective of Christian ethics. This was such an unusual request that we couldn't resist! The resulting conference was called "Environmental decision-making. Does theology help?" It involved engineers, environmental scientists, ethicists and theologians. We worked through a process of decision-making based on a Christian world view that had at its centre God's redemptive love for people and planet. Any decisions had to take into account the well-being of all of God's creation and not just be for human benefit.

The barrage, if built, could provide energy for the whole of South Wales but would make significant environmental changes to the Severn Estuary. We discovered that these changes were already happening (probably due to climate change) and the present ecosystem would not remain the same. The barrage would probably increase biodiversity, though this would not feature the familiar coastal wading birds that we now have. Our ethical model guided us to conclude that, if we sought to balance the needs of both people and the rest of nature, the barrage was still a possible choice to make. Clearly, far more detailed study would be needed to work out whether it really would be a good decision.

Westmill Wind Farm Co-operative

Adam Twine is a farmer who has been working to establish a community wind farm on an old airfield on the Oxfordshire/Wiltshire border for fifteen years. Here he tells his story.

Westmill Co-op[17] was set up in June 2005 to take forward the building of a wind farm on the airfield. It was established by two directors of Baywind (the first wind farm co-op in the UK) and Energy 4 All (an offshoot of Baywind promoting community-owned wind farms in the UK), and myself. In November 2006 Westmill launched a share prospectus in order both to raise the £4.3 million capital required and to give local people the opportunity to invest in the wind farm. The share offer achieved its target of £4.3 million with just over 2,000 members investing an average of £2,000 (with a minimum of £250 and a maximum of £20,000 per investor). Approximately half the members of Westmill live within a 30 km radius of the site.

Construction of the wind farm began in August 2007 and commissioning is due in March 2008. The struggle to achieve Westmill has been a rollercoaster for over fifteen years of work (far too long). It has taken such a long time partly because it was a pioneer in several significant areas: first wind farm in central England; first community wind farm to be set up from scratch; first co-op to attempt to raise £4.3 million in a share offer. Other difficulties resulted from the lack of national legislation to properly encourage renewables, and from a relatively small but well-resourced and well-connected opposition during the planning process. That it has succeeded is a testimony to the commitment and hard work put in by some key individuals and also the very tangible support from a large number of people who believed in the vision.

Biomass and biofuels

Biomass is essentially plant material such as wood and leaves, and biofuels are liquids such as bioethanol that are derived from plant material. People have been using biomass for energy since they invented fire, and so it is not at all new. In some parts of the developing world it is the major source of energy. For instance, in Sri Lanka 55% of energy is provided from biomass. However, until relatively recently it has been out of favour in the industrialized nations. All that has begun to change with climate change and the search for "carbon neutral" energy. Essentially, burning plant material is just putting back into the atmosphere carbon dioxide that the plants had taken out. Of course there will be some energy used to harvest and transport the biomass, but provided the site where it is burned is not too far away, then it is a relatively environmentally friendly option.[18] The big snag is the large amount of land that is needed, and it is estimated that to produce enough energy for the UK the whole land surface area would need to be planted with willow.[19]

The UK Government, however, sees a major future for biomass and biofuels, releasing its UK Biomass Strategy[20] on the same day as the Energy White Paper in 2007: "We will seek to deliver an expansion of biomass production in a way which is consistent with an enhanced, sustainable approach to land management." By 2020 they would see 17% of arable land being given over to biomass and biofuel production. The Biomass Strategy also sees potential in recovering more wood for energy use from currently unmanaged woodlands. The UK government has a fairly realistic approach to biofuels, and is aware of the potential environmental pitfalls. Unfortunately, in some parts of the world the growing of biofuel crops is already encountering environmental problems, and in some cases these crops are pushing up food prices.

Nuclear energy
Of course nuclear energy remains a very controversial energy option, at least with most environmental activists.

In 2007, nuclear power generates 18% of the UK's electricity. The UK Government, in its Energy White Paper, has given out strong signals that it might be in favour of building new nuclear power stations to replace the ageing stock. The reason appears to be that "the Government believes that giving energy companies the option of investing in new nuclear power stations lowers the costs and risks associated with achieving our energy goals to tackle climate change and ensure energy security".[21] Although the UK government considers that it might be able to meet its own target of a 60% reduction in carbon emissions by 2050 without nuclear power, doing so would not be as certain. There is a very long lead-in time to build a new nuclear power station, and the White Paper suggests that new stations could not make a contribution to Britain's energy supply until at least 2020. Inevitably, opposition focuses on nuclear waste disposal, potential accidents, nuclear proliferation and pollution. Those in favour of the nuclear option (probably) correctly point out that far more lives have already been lost due to the effects of climate change than can be attributed to nuclear power. The UK government is currently engaging in a public consultation on nuclear power. For me this is a difficult issue to call. Instinctively, I do not feel comfortable with nuclear power, but I have a strong suspicion that we may need it.

Personal carbon allowances or carbon taxes?

What tools do governments have that will encourage people to decrease their carbon emissions? In February 2007, I (Martin) was invited to attend a meeting in London, organized by the Environmental Change Institute of Oxford University[22] to look at how trials might be set up to investigate the running of Personal Carbon Allowance (PCA) schemes.[23] There were representatives of DEFRA,[24] local government and NGOs, and, as is frequently the case,

I was there as the delegate of the "faith communities". Put simply, PCA schemes would allow each person a certain amount of carbon to "spend" during an allotted period. So, for instance, if you wanted to take a flight or heat your home you would need both money and carbon credits. You would probably carry a carbon credit card to pay for your carbon usage, and you might buy additional credits from people who are lower users by logging on to a special Internet site. The advantage of PCA schemes is that they are equitable. The disadvantage is that they are complex. Do children get an allowance, and, if so, how much? Would elderly or vulnerable people be able to comprehend or use the system? If two people are travelling in a car, whose carbon allowance is used, the driver or the person paying for the petrol, or both? Two recent books come to very different conclusions regarding PCA schemes. Spencer and White[25] say that they "remain one of the most promising means of addressing the problems ... in a way that is consonant with biblical teaching". Goodall,[26] however, believes these schemes are "an elegant and completely impractical solution". Obviously there are many issues to think through concerning PCA, but governments are beginning to take this idea seriously as a future option.

The other major scheme for pressurizing people into using less fossil fuel is carbon taxation. This is much simpler to implement, but less fair. So if a government imposed a 50% carbon tax on petrol, the rich would probably keep driving as they could still afford to pay, but the poor would be prevented from doing so.[27] It is not yet clear which option individual governments will adopt, but no government will adopt a measure that disadvantages its people compared with those of other nations. We will return to this issue in Chapter 9, when we consider Contraction and Convergence.

To conclude this section, it is now evident that with climate change and Peak Oil both likely to hit this century there is a need for major change in our energy patterns. Governments will have a major role in this, as they will in deciding our transport options. We will look at these next.

Transport policies

When we have to travel into London from Oxford, we are faced with the choice of going by car, by train or by coach. For many years our preferred option has been the coach. The major snags with cars in London have been congestion and finding anywhere to park. Once you are on a coach you have a guaranteed seat. Unfortunately, at present, the trains into London are often overpacked, meaning an uncomfortable journey standing up. The coaches did have to deal with major congestion (average speeds in London were as low as 7 mph). Then, in February 2003, London mayor Ken Livingstone introduced congestion charging. His aims were to decrease the number of private cars in London, to reduce congestion, and to obtain finance for improvements to public transport. Each chargeable vehicle was required to pay £8 per day for entering the Central London area. Of course this was a highly controversial policy, with much opposition, but it worked for us.[28] The coaches now usually glide in and out of London with minimal delays! It is this kind of problem that governments have to deal with. Often there are many competing interests and priorities to address before a decision can be made, and often the eventual decision is unpopular with some section of society. If, however, governments can make public transport a comfortable, convenient and cheap option then they are onto a winner for the environment.

Simon Collings was a member of Sage in its very early days, and is a self-employed sustainable transport consultant.[29] He advises businesses on how they can reduce the environmental footprint of their transport operations. Here he looks at what will be needed in the 21st century.

Sustainable transport in the 21st century

When I started working as a sustainable transport consultant back in 1993, I would often be met with a perplexed look when people asked what I did. Occasionally someone would vaguely get it and declare that they used unleaded petrol, without realizing that almost all petrol was unleaded. How times have changed. Today, when asked the same question, I'm met with a much more enthusiastic and educated response, often ending up in a discussion about hybrid cars and whether biofuels are good or bad. But, although public awareness of the environmental impacts of transport is so much greater than it was fifteen years ago, there is still a long way to go before governments and citizens come to terms with what's really required to arrive at a truly sustainable transport system. If we are to reduce carbon emissions by 60% by 2050 from 1990 levels (as climate scientists say we need to), then we need to achieve an awful lot more than encouraging people to buy hybrid cars or whatever the latest available "technical fix" is. Technical solutions for transport emissions are important, but they are not the panacea many governments are banking on. Unless we tackle vehicle usage then transport emissions will remain too high. Reducing travel demand is the key challenge for delivering a sustainable transport system in the 21st century. Politicians must use environmental taxation to reduce demand for air travel and make public transport relatively cheaper than car travel (see photos 24 and 25). Managers must address their travel-intensive businesses in a globalized economy, as consumers start voting with their feet (or bicycles!). And individuals must question their travel patterns and start acting locally when it comes to shopping, leisure and work. Tackling vehicle (and aircraft) demand is a hard sell as it forces us to face up to our responsibilities. Hard maybe, but necessary, as technology alone is unlikely to deliver the emissions reductions we need.

Moses: Changing into the people of God

Moses was a leader for change. He had vision to inspire people and the faith to lead them forward. In the journey to the Promised Land, Moses encountered serious difficulties in gaining the commitment of his people to the vision of being the people of God. It took years of wandering in the wilderness for the complete vision to be accepted, and for the people to be ready to enter the Promised Land.

One of the classic change models was developed by Everett Rogers in the early 1960s.[30] He proposed that new ideas were diffused through populations of people by innovators who were pioneers of the change. This model sheds some light on the leadership of the Exodus and entering the Promised Land. It presupposes that there is a positive direction to lead people towards, and sets out to define different ways in which people will respond. First there are pioneers; like Moses and Aaron. These are the people who have the vision for change and will seek to lead others towards it. After that there are early adopters, the majority and late adopters. These will adopt the change but at different paces. Finally, there are laggards. These resist change and will oppose it. The skill of leadership is to shift thinking in preparation for change, so that there are many early adopters and very few laggards. When Moses first came down from Mount Sinai with the tablets of the Law (Exodus 32), he found his camp had rejected God and their journey. It took repentance and a reorientation of the people to recommit themselves to God and be prepared to follow Moses towards a very different life in the Promised Land. The reason for the early rejection can be understood by means of Rogers' ideas about the stages people go through in accepting a change. He saw five stages:[31]

1. Knowledge: learning about the existence and function of the innovation.

2. Persuasion: becoming convinced of the value of the innovation.

3. Decision: committing to the adoption of the innovation.

4. Implementation: putting it to use.

5. Confirmation: the ultimate acceptance (or rejection) of the innovation.

The story of the Exodus is about all these categories operating at different stages and being adopted at different paces. Because the change was a major one it was impossible to persuade people very quickly, but skilled leadership moved them progressively forward and gradually transformed them into the people of God.

Britain, along with other nations, is facing the need for change, and this is being reflected in some of the new legislation going through parliament on the issues we have addressed in this chapter. This legislation will need to be embraced at grass-roots level and will therefore need to be diffused by pioneers who are keen to lead the change. So to achieve its goals our government needs organizations that are connected to the national leadership initiatives, but have hands-on involvement in local communities. One group of organizations that are especially well placed to enable this change of thinking are the faith communities. Of these, the churches have a particularly strategic role because they are the largest group and have the widest national and international coverage.

National church's responsibility for environment

Church denominations at a national level are increasingly taking environmental issues seriously, and many have detailed environmental policy statements. For instance, statements are available for the Methodist Church[32] and the United Reformed Church,[33] both in the UK. Similarly, the Catholic Church in England and Wales produced "The Call of Creation: God's Invitation and the Human Response" in 2002.[34] In the Church of England, it is now relatively common for bishops and other senior figures to make statements about environmental issues. At the General Synod of November 2005, the Archbishop of Canterbury, Rowan Williams, said of the environmental crisis that "it is probably the most urgent public moral issue of our time". At the synod the delegates discussed a report that had been put together by Clare Foster, the Archbishop's adviser on the environment.[35]

In most cases, at least in the UK, the national denominational organizations seem to set overall policy directions on the environment, but leave individual congregations to sort out implementation. They often recommend Eco-Congregation (see Chapter 7) or materials from other organizations. The Church of England, however, decided to take more direct action through its "Shrinking the Footprint" campaign.[36] This commits the Church to becoming a "40% Church" by 2050, slashing its carbon emissions. Its first project was to conduct a baseline survey of carbon emissions for churches in 2005. The aim is to repeat this at regular intervals in order to assess how much progress has been made in reducing emissions. To help churches become more environmentally friendly, two small guidebooks have been produced.[37] The Episcopal Church of the USA (ECUSA) has taken a similar route to the Church of England, and has set up the Episcopal Ecological Network (EpEN) to co-ordinate its environmental work.[38]

National Christian environmental organizations

Although many church denominations are involved in Christian environmental work at a national level, undoubtedly much more activity is generated by a variety of non-denominational para-church organizations. Two very different groups are described below, and the work of several more is described in other chapters (for a complete listing, see our Useful Websites section at the end of the book).

In 1981 some Christian delegates met informally for prayer at a Green Party conference in the UK. As a result, Christian Ecology Link (CEL) was founded in 1982, and has since grown into an organization of some 850 members.[39] It celebrated its 25th birthday in July 2007, when it held the "Storm of Hope" conference in London. CEL "offers insights into ecology and the environment to Christian people and churches and offers Christian insights to the Green movement". Mobilizing Christians to campaign for practical responses to key issues is central to CEL's approach. CEL has been the driving force behind the climate change campaign Operation Noah,[40] and the LOAF food campaign (see Chapter 6).

The Evangelical Environmental Network (EEN)[41] from North America was founded on 31 October 1994, and is a network of individuals and organizations whose aim is to "declare the Lordship of Christ over all creation" (Colossians 1:15–20). EEN publishes *Creation Care* magazine, and was very much involved in the formulation of the Evangelical Declaration on the Care of Creation in 1994.[42] We will return to this in Chapter 10. Another high-profile

EEN campaign is entitled "What Would Jesus Drive?" which was intended to help Christians focus on their transportation choices.

Change as transformation

The greatest change of all history was the resurrection of Jesus from the dead. Jesus transformed despair into hope, and sadness into joy. He did not do this by intellectual debate, or by inspiring people to reach higher spiritual realms, but by physically rising from the dead. Like the incarnation of Christ, the resurrection is the ultimate affirmation of the importance of this world. Leadership for change is essentially narrative. Leaders need to provide a fresh story that will enable people to move forward to a vision of a better future.[43] In the resurrection of Jesus we have that vision. As we grasp the significance of Christ's defeat of death and redemption of the cosmos, so we can gain the courage to follow the way of Christ in our care for people and planet. This will lead to a simpler lifestyle for ourselves, and to a commitment to equality and sharing with those in need – both nations and individuals. It will also lead to a concern for the non-human inhabitants of our Earth and their precious habitats. The goal we look towards is of a life that is simpler but of far greater quality. This new style of living will be more "earthed" in a commitment to our world, but more deeply spiritual in our understanding of the creation and our creator.

Having looked at national issues in the West and the need to have leadership for change, we will now consider the situation in the less developed countries, often still known as the Third World.

9

Uniting with the Global South

The great battleground for the defence and expansion of freedom today is the whole southern half of the globe – Asia, Latin America, Africa and the Middle East – the lands of the rising peoples. Their revolution is the greatest in human history. They seek an end to injustice, tyranny, and exploitation. More than an end, they seek a beginning.

John F. Kennedy (1917-1963)[1]

In the late 1980s I (Margot) went to study at All Nations, an international Christian college with students of over 35 nationalities.[2] I became friends with an African couple, Hilkiah and Martha Omindo from Tanzania. Hilkiah was an Anglican priest and he went on to become Bishop of Mara on the shores of Lake Victoria. I learnt much about the African church from the Omindos.

Bishop Hilkiah wrote recently to describe the environmental projects in his diocese:[3]

Tree-planting in Tanzania
The Anglican Church of Tanzania Diocese of Mara is situated between the shores of Lake Victoria in the west and the Serengeti National Park in the east. Therefore part of it is on the plains of the national park, which is dry land. Here there has been extensive deforestation resulting from human activity and also from wild animals, such as

elephants. The impact of deforestation is very negative on the lives of people and animals. The amount of rainfall we used to get when we had trees around has reduced and we now receive one-third of our usual rainfall, and as a result we don't get a good harvest. When we were growing up we did not see hunger, but now small children know about hunger because they have encountered it in their lives. The freshwater springs that used to help people have dried up and the women now have to walk miles to fetch water. They do this with their children on their back because the older ones have gone to school and the men have gone to find food. The dry heat is hard on the mother and the child and so both of them are punished because of deforestation. Food has become scarce and expensive and malnutrition is on our doorstep. We use firewood for cooking, and therefore the deforestation also means that we lack fuel. This is another punishment for the woman and her child because she has to go miles to try to get firewood.

Our Diocese is holistic in its mission and we do development work alongside discipleship. We already have three programmes, which have tree-planting as part of their activities together with agriculture, livestock, water and improved homes. These are Buhemba Rural Agricultural Centre, Mogabiri Farmers Extension Centre, and the Integrated Community Development Programme. But in October 2007 we are planning to have a new programme on tree-planting, which is run by the Mothers' Union, and the target group is the women. We want the women to have woodlots around their homes to help them with firewood and to reforest the area. We will encourage the use of fuel-efficient stoves, which will be made locally. We have already planted some trees through the above programmes but now I think involving the women will be more effective. The woodlots will be around the homesteads and they can take care of them. If we manage to have woodlots at every home, we can claim back our rainfall, which has gone to England![4]

A world without rest

The impact of environmental degradation on the women of Mara has been a loss of rest. This pattern is repeated around the globe as people compete for increasingly scarce resources. Men, women, children and also other species struggle to survive in ever more hostile environments. Meanwhile, in the wealthy parts of the world, there also seems little rest, as our cities "stay open" 24/7 and there is pressure to work ever harder for more material wealth.

The concept of Sabbath is a protest against the injustice of overwork. We find from Genesis 2:2 that it was built into the very fabric of creation. God's work was completed only on the seventh day when he rested.[5] So for humans and all creation, this rest is needed for our own well-being. As Sabbath thinking developed in the Bible, it became a means of ensuring justice for the more vulnerable in society. In the Ten Commandments (Exodus 20:8–11) it was the responsibility of the heads of household to provide this rest for their families, their workers, the poor and animals. Strangers too should be given rest. It is a gift that should be available to all. A commitment to Sabbath had to be collective. It is easy for the powerful to take rest at the expense of others. Conscious effort is needed to give a fair rest to all.

Today our lives interconnect around the globe and the choices we make have a direct impact on the lives of others. Buying cheap clothing made in the Far East may be taking Sabbath and a decent wage away from other humans. Buying cheap products made of tropical hardwoods, or overfishing some species such as cod, may be taking

Sabbath away from our biodiversity, which is unable to recover from the high levels of exploitation. We need to act to implement Sabbath as a justice principle for our global community. The life of our planet needs a new beginning.

Globalization and the poor

Whether we like it or not, much of the material we have covered in this book has been, and still is, affected by the all-pervasive phenomenon of globalization. Globalization has many different aspects, including economic, political, cultural and ideological, and a good overall definition is:

> Globalization refers to a multidimensional set of social processes that create, multiply, stretch and intensify worldwide social interdependencies and exchanges while at the same time fostering in people a growing awareness of deepening connections between the local and the distant.[6]

In other words, our local environment, in its widest sense, is being affected to a far greater extent by distant governments, organizations and processes than it was say 100 years ago.

The term "global village" was first coined by Marshall McLuhan in 1962.[7] He foresaw the Internet and the increase in global communications that this would allow. Our world has become smaller as transport has speeded up and become relatively cheaper and modern media have enabled so many methods of instant communication. Not everyone is a great fan of globalization, however, as is shown by the large numbers of protesters who appear at the International Monetary Fund (IMF), World Bank and G8 meetings around the world. One of the strange features of globalization is that many of the protest groups will have used the Internet to mobilize their supporters, and mobile phones to keep in touch with each other during demonstrations, and so are using the products of globalization to attack globalization. But one does not have to be an anti-globalization protester to have the feeling that there are some aspects of globalization we could do without. Possibly the most disturbing feature is the rise of large multinational companies. These are very difficult to regulate, and if they do not like the laws or economic conditions of one country they have a tendency to move elsewhere. They are thus effectively free from democratic control.

We live in a world of huge inequality and this is now visible to those with the least as well as to those with the most. The bulk of population growth has happened in the poorer countries of the world.[8] Higher population means less land per family in rural areas and more crowding and poverty in the cities. Added to this are climate change issues, HIV/Aids and other health problems, political instability and the economic dominance of the wealthy nations. The daily reality for many people in poorer countries is bleak. In our global village people living in a few nations live lifestyles that would have been reserved for only the very rich of previous generations. Meanwhile, the majority face abject poverty. Like a feudal village of old, the rich live in comfortable homes and many aspects of their lives are sustained by the poorly paid labour of the majority. Everything from electronics to kitchenware seems to be produced in low-income countries that may lack the strict employment and safety laws of Europe or North America. In Britain we now find we can have luxury vegetables, fruit and cut flowers all year round. These are flown in from Africa – sometimes from countries that are themselves facing food shortages. It is not easy for people to know whether to buy these products to boost the economies of these countries, or to boycott them because they perpetuate poor factory conditions and use land that was used for local food production. Our global village is spinning out of control, and our shrunken world is struggling to support the growing demands of humans. How should we respond?

Rich Christians in an age of hunger

One of the first Christian books written about the contemporary problem of world inequality was *Rich Christians in an Age of Hunger* by Ronald Sider.[9] When it came out it had a huge impact on many Christians who had previously been unaware of just how great world inequality was and of the serious malnutrition problem faced by much of the world. Sider advocated three things. Firstly, we should aim at a simpler personal lifestyle to symbolize and facilitate a concern for the hungry. He encouraged the principle of sharing (2 Corinthians 8:14) and a biblical standard of simply seeking to have "enough" (2 Corinthians 9:8). Secondly, he advocated a different way of Christian living that was far more communal and open to the needy. Thirdly, he advocated the changing of unjust structures in society, and saw this as a prophetic call on the church. In the foreword to the UK edition, the Revd David Watson said: "This book contains the most vital challenge which faces the church of today... it calls, above all, for immediate and sacrificial action, if we know anything of God's love in our hearts."[10]

Sabbath and Jubilee years

Sider looked at the biblical theme of Jubilee. This can be found in Leviticus 25 and is part of the teaching on Sabbath and rest. In addition to a weekly Sabbath for humans and animals, there is also provision for a Sabbath for the land. Leviticus 25:1–6 describes this Sabbath as every seventh year. The land must be allowed to rest and not be sown or harvested, and vineyards must not be pruned. Farmers can go to their fields to gather enough for their daily needs from what has grown up naturally, but their fields should be left open to allow the poor to glean as well. The Sabbath year is to remind us that land is a gift from God in creation and should be held in trust, because we do not own it. We also remember that rest is a part of the creative process and all parts of God's creation need to experience it to maintain their fruitfulness.[11]

In addition to the seven-year cycle of Sabbaths, every fiftieth year was a special Sabbath year known as the Jubilee. The Jubilee year was not only a Sabbath rest for the fields and the people, but a year to release prisoners, cancel debts and return land to its historic owners. This did not deny people the opportunity of becoming successful but it made sure that the negative consequences of inequality were limited by this redistribution system. Sider described Leviticus 25 as "one of the most radical texts in all of Scripture"[12] because the Jubilee provided institutionalized justice, which would happen automatically. Unlike charitable handouts, the return of land was the right of the poor and would give them back the means of earning their own income again. The Jubilee Year was inaugurated on the Day of Atonement, when people were able to restore their relationship with God through sacrifice, prayer and repentance. When we put this in the context of the three-way relationship between God, people and the rest of nature[13] we realize that beginning the Jubilee on the Day of Atonement is significant because reconciliation with God is essential if there is to be reconciliation with other humans and with the Earth.

Jubilee and the debt campaigns

Many people still associate the word "Jubilee" with the Jubilee 2000 "drop the debt" campaign in the 1990s.[14] This was an international movement that campaigned for a cancellation of the debts of the poorest countries at the millennium. One of their most visible events was the 70,000-strong human chain around the venue for the G8 Summit in May 1998. The background to this campaign was the severe debt that many countries had found themselves in, with no hope of repayment. Debt repayments from some nations amounted to more than the aid they were receiving from the wealthier countries. The cost in human suffering has been immense, with money diverted from educational and medical projects. There has also been an environmental cost as countries have sought to exploit their natural resources to the full to pay off the interest on their loans.

Debt, the World Bank and economic solutions

World debt is a very complex problem and many factors have influenced the current world situation. In part it originated as profits were made from rising oil prices in the 1970s. This meant that wealthier nations had money that they wished to invest, and looked to the "least developed countries" (LDCs) as potential targets for loans. As world interest rates went up in the 1980s these debts mushroomed and became unpayable for many low-income countries. These countries sought to raise money through exports of basic commodities such as coffee, cocoa and cotton. In the 1990s the collapse in the prices of these primary goods meant that their debt grew ever larger.[15]

The World Bank and the IMF sought to tackle the situation by introducing Structural Adjustment Programmes (SAPs). These programmes required countries to cut public spending and open their internal markets to free trade. This was an attempt to place LDCs on a stronger financial footing. Sadly, many cut programmes in education and health, which had a very negative impact on their citizens. As the trade barriers of these countries were removed, fledgling industries found themselves competing with major multinationals and were not able to survive.

In some places the environmental impact has been severe. Multinational companies relocated their industries to countries with little or no environmental legislation. Those critical of these companies claim that this has meant that goods are produced with scant regard to local and regional pollution, and with completely unsustainable use of natural resources. Forests have been cleared, and more intensive farming on previously uncultivated land has led to soil erosion. Rivers have been polluted, and land damaged through mining. Local people have found themselves paying the environmental price, while the majority of the profits go elsewhere. A Dutch-led study showed SAPs had some positive effects but these were far outweighed by negative impacts.[16]

Naboth's vineyard and the consequences to the rich of oppressing the poor

The biblical story of Naboth in 1 Kings 21 highlights the injustice of the rich taking natural resources that rightfully belong to the poor. Naboth was killed on the strength of a false accusation because he refused to sell his family vineyard to the king for use as a vegetable garden. Naboth took seriously the Jubilee teaching that land was a gift from God and was held in trust. He paid for his principles with his life, but the king's descendants had to face the consequences of this injustice and eventually disaster fell on their heads. Today we are beginning to understand the interconnectedness of our world and the consequences of our overuse of resources. Like Naboth, the poor are suffering from the greed of the rich and all our descendants will face the negative consequences.

The goals for poverty, development and the future

As the year 2000 approached, the widening gap between the rich and the poor became apparent. Between 1960 and 2000, some parts of Asia became wealthier and did begin to "catch up" with the richer countries. In sub-Saharan Africa and the LDCs, however, there was a dramatic widening of the gap: whereas in 1960 a person in one of these countries would earn one-tenth of someone in the West, by 2000 that had shrunk to only one-twentieth.[17] A further study concluded that the top 1% of the world's population had as much wealth as the bottom 57%.[18] In the light of this growing disparity the UN General Assembly in 2000 adopted a Millennium Declaration to set goals to reduce poverty. This declaration set the following goals:

Millennium Declaration Goals

• Halving the proportion of the world's people suffering from poverty and hunger

• Achieving universal completion of primary school education

• Promoting gender equality access to education and empowering women

• Reducing under-five mortality rates by two-thirds

• Reducing maternal mortality rates by three-quarters

• Halting and beginning to reverse the spread of HIV/AIDS, malaria and other major diseases

• Ensuring environmental sustainability

• Developing a global partnership for development

These goals provide a laudable list of issues that have immediate impact on human suffering. Two things are weak: firstly, alongside commitments to reduce mortality there is no commitment to reduce birth rates.[19] Unless this is tackled the disparity between rich and poor will inevitably increase. Secondly, the lack of understanding of the interconnectedness between human and environmental concerns is apparent in the imbalance between human and environmental goals.

These omissions are not new. In 1972, the Limits to Growth study[20] suggested aiming at zero population and economic growth, but was heavily criticized. The UN Stockholm conference at this time advocated prudence in our use of finite environmental resources, but this prudence was seen as conflicting with human concerns and an obstacle to the alleviation of poverty. Challenges came from the World Conservation Strategy in the 1970s and the Brundtland Report, *Our Common Future*, in 1987.[21] In 1992, the Earth Summit at Rio de Janeiro sought to find a balance between human and environmental needs. It defined sustainable development as "improving the quality of human life while living within the carrying capacity of supporting ecosystems".[22]

The UN had produced a set of International Development Targets in the late 1990s that included environmental targets, but these were not developed significantly with the Millennium Goals. Thankfully now, seven years on, environmental concerns are being considered seriously by some concerned about development and world poverty, but population is still too controversial a subject to be addressed seriously by many, even though it is a driving force for poverty, hunger and environmental degradation.

The impact of climate change on Africa and Asia

In Chapter 3 we considered climate change in general terms, and noted that it would be likely to have a disproportionate effect on the world's poor countries, but what will those effects be?

The IPCC report in 2007 has suggested a rise in sea level of 28-43 cm by 2100. This does not sound very much, but 10 million people in Bangladesh alone live between 0 and 1 metre above sea level. So any increase in sea level will only exacerbate problems caused by episodes of heavy rain.

As the global temperature increases, some areas will be worse affected than others. Unfortunately, it looks as if Africa will be particularly badly hit. More worrying than the temperature increase is that we are expecting an increase in floods and droughts. It seems likely that already wet areas may get wetter, and that drought-stricken zones may get even drier.[23] As we write this section, in August 2007, it is only a month since parts of Oxford were flooded, and agriculture was very badly affected in a number of the southern counties of England (see Chapter 8). Now, however, reports are coming in of far more serious floods in large areas of Asia, including India, Bangladesh and Nepal. These are probably the worst for 30 years. The death toll is mounting, and will almost certainly reach thousands. Some people are surviving by eating snails and rats, and, because the water supplies have often become contaminated, diseases and diarrhoea are rife.

In 2007 floods have also affected Africa, including countries such as Sudan, Mali and Gambia. However, Africa is probably better known for droughts and the resulting famines, and several southern African countries have suffered in this way in 2007. For example, tiny Lesotho has had the worst drought in 30 years, and the maize harvest was down by more than 40%. Bishop Hilkiah's story at the beginning of this chapter highlights drought in Tanzania, and this is true for other East African countries. In 2006 the autumn rains in Rwanda failed, destroying the vital second crop for families.[24]

Warmer and wetter conditions will result in increased

health risks from diseases borne by parasites. An obvious one is malaria, but other tropical diseases will also spread geographically.[25] Again, Sub-Saharan Africa looks likely to be particularly badly affected.

The effects of increased temperatures, sea-level rise, floods, droughts and increased health risks from disease are likely to be very serious, and they will almost inevitably lead to a major refugee problem. Norman Myers has estimated that in 1995 there were 25 million environmental refugees, that the figure will double by 2010, and that when global warming really takes hold there could be as many as 200 million.[26] Sadly, and inevitably, most of those refugees will be from developing countries.

Christian development agencies

The Christian relief agency Tearfund has engaged significantly with environmental issues as a result of climate change. They take a holistic approach, seeking to combine care for the environment with a concern for the poor. They see their environmental work as "part of their God-given responsibility for Creation and ... essential practically for lifting people out of poverty".[27] Examples of Tearfund's approaches are minimum-tillage farming in the Monze East area of Zambia, and the restoration of "bunds" (earth walls) around fields in Rajasthan, India. Both approaches reduce soil erosion and improve the fertility of the soil. Bunds also help to conserve water. In the UK, Tearfund are working with churches and individuals to decrease carbon usage.

Christian Aid became concerned about environmental issues when they saw the negative impacts of climate change on many of the communities in low-income countries.[28] They predict that efforts to reduce poverty through development work and debt campaigns could be wiped out by the problems caused by global warming.

Environment and development

Climate change has led many development agencies to take a more holistic approach to their work, but some still work primarily from an anthropocentric perspective. Likewise, many environmental agencies take human need into account with their projects, but their key concerns remain environmental, whether ecocentric or biocentric. James Pender is an environmental scientist, working in a development programme in Bangladesh with the Church Mission Society.[29] He recently spent a study leave with us to reflect on this issue, and he outlines his conclusions and how a holistic theocentric approach[30] can provide a way forward.

A holistic approach in Bangladesh

Since I came to rural Bangladesh four years ago I have been working as a missionary adviser with the Church of Bangladesh Social Development Programme (CBSDP). Here, unlike in Western countries, the link between development, poverty and the environment is easily understood. In Bangladesh, the most densely populated country on Earth, 80% of its 150 million people still live in rural areas and mostly work in agriculture. A poor family in the flood-prone south or the drought-prone north does not see climate change as an issue for environmentalists, but as a direct threat to their survival, as these climate related disasters are already becoming more frequent and severe (see photo 26). Our programme for combating drought by planting shelter belts of trees along roads (to increase local humidity and reduce the drying effect of wind) will benefit wildlife and people. Likewise, a herbal doctor in Modhupur forest talked of deforestation not in terms of biodiversity loss but as a threat to his community's health, as vital medicinal plants are lost. Our medicinal plant project will therefore benefit species preservation and community health. It is very hard to separate out which of our activities are social and which are environmental. The distribution of over 20,000 fruit, medicinal and timber trees per year to poor households in Meherpur District will mitigate global warming by absorbing carbon dioxide, but will also improve nutrition, health and income.

Promotion of organic farming blurs the boundaries even further. The fish stocks it will preserve by preventing "algal bloom" due to fertilizer run-off are a vital source of protein for villagers. It will also help conservation of Hilsha, the "national fish", which has declined by 66% in the last fifteen years. We are investigating techniques that use compost or nitrifying bacteria (biofertilizer) to see if they increase farmers' yields and profits. I have learned that it is the poor who are most dependent on good healthy ecosystems. Development that damages the environment also destroys the livelihoods of the poor. As we seek to serve the poor we must conserve and enrich the natural resource base on which they depend if they are to prosper (see photos 27 and 28). The rural communities in Bangladesh know this already, but it is a truth that so-called "developed" countries must also urgently learn.

Blessings and warnings

The holistic nature of human and environmental concerns is reflected in the implications of responsible and irresponsible lifestyles set out in Leviticus 26. This passage points to interconnectedness between people and the earth, and the Jubilee theme is also woven into the warnings (26:34-35). Dislocation from God will lead to dislocation from the fruits of nature. The result of irresponsible lifestyles will be a loss of land that will then "enjoy its Sabbath years" while the people are in exile. Each year we release the carbon of about a million years of photosynthesis.[31] This means that our generation has consumed the harvests of millions of years of the Earth's fruitfulness. This is not stewardship but exploitation, and cannot continue. Unless we begin to call a halt, the Earth's systems, in adapting to a changed atmosphere, will leave many places uninhabitable for humans. It will be given its Sabbath rests.

Appropriate technology and appropriate development

We mentioned in Chapter 6 that in 2002 we visited the Asian Rural Institute (ARI)[32] in Japan. While there, we were shown an experimental rice paddy field grown under a novel cultivation method known as the System of Rice Intensification (SRI). Staff at ARI claimed that SRI could give greatly improved yields. I (Martin) made a mental note to check this out when I returned to the UK. After all, I am a curious scientist. Little did I expect that I would be entering a scientific war zone!

SRI was originally developed 20 years ago in Madagascar by Father Henri de Laulanié, a Jesuit priest. In SRI, rice seedlings are transplanted when as young as twelve days old, the plants are spaced widely apart, and the rice fields should be kept moist but not flooded. At least in Madagascar the results were astounding, with yields increasing two- to threefold. Norman Uphoff of Cornell University in the United States got involved, and has been the most passionate advocate of SRI.[33] Not all scientists were convinced, however, and John Sheehy, of the International Rice Research Institute (IRRI) in the Philippines, conducted a series of careful experiments which suggested that SRI was not significantly better in yield than conventionally grown rice. The battle between Uphoff and Sheehy was well illustrated when it appeared in the top scientific journal, *Nature*, in 2004.[34] There is no doubt that SRI is proving very popular throughout the developing world, with thousands of farms switching to it. The most recent work, however, suggests that, apart from in Madagascar, yields are not increased using SRI, and may even be decreased.[35] Even if this is the case, the plants grown under SRI use considerably less water, which may be an overriding factor in many locations. SRI is an example of appropriate technology, and is something that rice farmers can try without having to rely on funds, seed, chemicals or equipment from elsewhere.

The battle over SRI is a microcosm of a war that is going on around the world. On the one side we have organic agriculture, "local" and anti-globalization, and on the other the multinational agrichemical companies and the forces of globalization. My personal feeling is that SRI probably does "work" in some climatic and some soil conditions. I am certain, however, that the amount of money going into research on SRI is far less than that going into other rice research, genetically modified "golden rice," for instance. We will return to this in Chapter 10.

Modernization in Zanskar

A further complex area in finding the balance between local "low-tech" ways of increasing yields and external scientific solutions is the use of inorganic fertilizers. One of Martin's former students, Seb Mankelow, is an environmental scientist and trek leader who frequently visits Zanskar. He reflects on the effects of modernization there, and the need to be open-minded about the potential positive and negative impacts.

Zanskar's agriculture – Seb Mankelow

On the northern slopes of India's Greater Himalaya, the Zanskar Valley exists at the periphery of 21st-century India (see photo 29). I have been observing changes in this region annually since 1994, and Zanskar's development has helped broaden my outlook from that of a countercultural mountaineer to someone who accepts that modernization in remote areas is not always something to be avoided. My research in the area has focused on agricultural change and a shift in fertilizer practice from the application of animal dung and night soil to the additional application of inorganic fertilizer. Often considered detrimental to long-term agricultural productivity, inorganic fertilizers are frequently linked to a decline in soil structure and the depletion of soil micronutrients. Encouraged by subsidy and government departments, inorganic fertilizers have been trialled by a number of Zanskar's farmers and many have confirmed that increased yields are short-term. Environmental NGOs have been quick to highlight these shortcomings, yet few have taken the time to investigate how the unorthodox application of inorganic fertilizers has been employed to offset labour and time shortages in Zanskar's agricultural communities. Through a process of trial and error, Zanskar's farmers have discovered that applying an excess of nitrogen cultivates a taller crop. Collecting this excess biomass from the threshing circle offsets the time and labour otherwise required to cut and transport winter fodder for livestock (see photo 30). The saving is significant, to the extent that many farmers would no longer consider growing barley without satisfying their fodder requirements from the same crop. Although in the short term this practice is proving beneficial, using inorganic fertilizer in this way is not a sustainable solution. It does, however, demonstrate the complex and unorthodox ways in which external technology is often integrated into remote communities; something often overlooked when trying to "save" remote cultures from the dangers of modernization.

Contraction and convergence

It will be impossible for developing countries to modernize without using more energy. Significant financial investment will be required if these new energy sources are to be renewable rather than carbon-based, and some will wish to use their own available fossil fuels. In Chapter 8 we saw that some governments are actively considering some form of carbon rationing for individuals, possibly a personal carbon allowance. Contraction and Convergence (C&C) is an extension of this idea to the international arena. The idea is relatively simple in principle, and was first proposed by Aubrey Meyer of the Global Commons Institute (GCI).[36] First, we need to agree on a level of carbon dioxide in the atmosphere as a target. Then we calculate how much carbon dioxide each person on the planet can be allowed if everyone is to have an equal share. Each country would be allowed this amount multiplied by the number of its citizens. If the target CO_2 concentration in the atmosphere was fixed at a level of 450 ppm by 2100 (the level suggested by GCI), this would undoubtedly mean that the Western industrialized nations would need to decrease their emissions very markedly. The developing nations would, however, have some room to increase their emissions to enable them to industrialize. If a nation wanted to emit more CO_2 than its target then it would have to buy credits from a country that was emitting less than its goal. So this is a just system, where everyone would be treated equally. Not surprisingly, many of the industrialized nations are not that keen, and the developing nations quite like the idea. Whether it will ever be implemented will depend on how much our governments pressurize the international community, and how much we pressurize our governments.[37]

Jesus and Jubilee

Contraction and Convergence operates a principle of fairness for nations and individuals and this links to the Jubilee theme of this chapter. Jubilee can be found in the Gospels as well as in the Old Testament. Not only was Jesus aware of the Jubilee in scripture, but he chose this to be the text of his first sermon as he set out on his mission:

> The Spirit of the Lord is on me,
> because he has anointed me
> to preach good news to the poor.
> He has sent me to proclaim freedom for the prisoners
> and recovery of sight for the blind,
> to release the oppressed,
> to proclaim the year of the Lord's favour. (Luke 4:18–19)

This passage is a quotation from Isaiah 61:1–2, and the phrase "Year of the Lord's Favour" is the literal meaning of "Year of Jubilee". The implication is clear: the new way of living that Jesus is outlining is one where we are called to live in Jubilee. It describes a kingdom where there is freedom and justice for all. Jesus is keen to bring out the fullest possible interpretation of this passage. The phrases "release of prisoners" and "giving sight to the blind" are alternative translations of the same verse in Isaiah 61. In providing the two interpretations, Jesus makes the point that both physical freedom and healing will be part of his mission.

Since this was how Jesus began his mission it is not surprising that, after the resurrection, the disciples want to know the full extent of the Jubilee to be inaugurated. At the start of the book of Acts, Luke records that the disciples ask if this is the time to restore the Kingdom to Israel (Acts 1:6). The disciples saw the reconnection of people and land as an essential part of the fulfilment of Jubilee. Jesus does not deny this, but simply states that their immediate task is to concentrate on proclaiming the message to the ends of the Earth.

Who are the poor, the oppressed and the suffering today? They would definitely be people in the global South. Could the land and its biodiversity also be described in this way? As Christians we preach our good news by proclaiming Jubilee, and our mission for this century is to find a way of combining a concern for the Earth and its people. We will continue to consider global issues in Chapter 10, and then in Chapter 11 will look to the future and when "the land will finally be restored".

10

Dreams and visions

> The answer depends on us. Even in a cosmic or geological time-perspective, there's something unique about our century: for the first time in its history, our entire planet's fate depends on human actions and human choices.
>
> Lord Rees of Ludlow[1]

Global rescue

Noah was a visionary. He is described as "a righteous man, blameless among the people of his time, and he walked with God" (Genesis 6:9). Few others in the Bible are described in quite such glowing terms and it is not surprising that God chose Noah to implement his rescue mission of righteous humans and world biodiversity. Noah's foresight and his obedience to God enabled him to save a whole generation of life on the planet.

In this chapter we will look at different organizations of importance on the environmental scene that have the vision to respond to global needs. We will highlight examples of government and church initiatives as well as scientific advances, particularly those sponsored by multinational organizations. Firstly we will tell the story of one Christian organization that came into being as a result of a vision to protect a vulnerable habitat in southern Portugal.

A Rocha

In the autumn of 1992 a group of Sage[2] members gathered to watch a video about a then almost unknown Christian environmental organization, A Rocha.[3] The video showed the work of A Rocha at their field centre in the Algarve in southern Portugal. Even in the early 1990s the Algarve was under threat from major tourist development, and the A Rocha centre, Cruzinha, was near the Alvor estuary, one of the last remaining unspoilt parts of the coastline. The Alvor estuary is a particularly important site for migratory birds, and much of A Rocha's work at the time concerned monitoring their populations and movements. One of the Sage group, Karl Wallendszus, was an old friend of Will Simonson,[4] one of the A Rocha staff workers in Portugal. Karl suggested that we should plan to visit the A Rocha centre in Portugal in April 1993. I (Martin[5]) don't think any of us quite realized what we were going to, or what influence A Rocha would have in the coming years.

On 1 April 1993 a party of six Sage members arrived at Faro airport in the Algarve. We were met there by Peter and Miranda Harris, the then directors of the A Rocha centre at Cruzinha.[6] We spent a week there getting to know the A Rocha staff, helping with some conservation projects, and generally finding out all there was to know about A Rocha. We came to know the moths, beetles, birds and flowers. We had daily Bible studies, and lots of walks and relaxation. We left Portugal determined to help A Rocha in as many ways as possible, and over the years we have.

For some years after our trip in 1993, A Rocha remained rooted in Portugal,[7] but towards the end of the 1990s other A Rocha projects started to spring up in Lebanon, Kenya, France and Canada. People who had visited the original A Rocha project in Portugal caught the vision, and soon there were a whole family of projects all over the world. More are on the way.

Although the original idea for A Rocha came out of the UK, and much of the early support for the centre in Portugal was British, it was not until 2001 that A Rocha UK was founded. It was not where anyone might have expected! For some years previously, Dave Bookless had been Anglican vicar of St George's in Southall, West London, one of the most multicultural areas in the UK. In 2000 Margot was training for the Anglican ministry, and decided to do one of her placements with Dave in Southall. Dave took her out onto the Minet site in Southall. Once part of the London heathland, it was now a rubbish dump and a site for car-boot sales. Motorbikes sped across the site churning up what remained of the soil. This, Dave explained, was going to be where A Rocha UK would start its work! Very rapidly, it did. In collaboration with the local community, the council and others, A Rocha UK set about reclaiming the Minet site. Over the years since 2001 we have been on a number of Sage and A Rocha visits to Southall, and have witnessed the transformation that has been brought about. On our last visit to a rainy Minet site, in June 2007, we had our farmer friend, John Neal,[8] with us. John, who knows more than any of us about tending the land, was just incredibly impressed.

Then things came full circle for us and for Sage. We returned to Cruzinha in April 2005, twelve years after our first visit (see photo 31). In 2006, rural vicar Simon Brignall approached A Rocha UK about setting up a project based at his church in Lewknor, 16 miles south-east of Oxford.[9] Simon soon came into the Sage network, and we helped in the planning of the opening (Environment Sunday) service for the project on 3 June 2007.[10] There in the congregation at the open-air service at Aston Rowant

National Nature Reserve near Lewknor were several of us who had been present at the first Sage meeting in 1990, and who had been on the visit to Portugal in 1993. Back in the church at Lewknor Dave Bookless gave the sermon.

What next for Sage? What next for A Rocha? One small local group and one international organization, both committed to the same ideals and to working together for God's creation. We would predict that A Rocha will continue to grow in both size and influence. Sage will probably stay the same, and carry on with its work in the Oxford area. At the last conservation work party at Boundary Brook we hatched a plan to write the history of Sage in time for the 20th anniversary in 2010; now there's an idea... Whatever the future, we are convinced that we need both more local groups like Sage and strong international organizations such as A Rocha.

Biblical husbandry

If Noah was the champion of animal protection in the Bible, Jacob was the pioneer in selective breeding (Genesis 27–35). Jacob dreamed of personal success. His methods of achieving this were often selfish and had negative repercussions on others and himself. He worked as a shepherd for his father-in-law, Laban, who allowed him to keep any spotted sheep for himself. Jacob set about breeding speckled rather than plain sheep and succeeded in this, despite that rather vague description of how he actually achieved it! Jacob gradually gained ownership of the majority of the herds belonging to Laban, who was forced to acknowledge the speckled sheep as Jacob's.

The contemporary dreams of many major companies involved in modern plant and animal "breeding" are focused on the potential of developing changes at the genetic level. Some scientists involved have a vision that their work will yet enable humanity to feed the world and make major medical advances. They are hugely frustrated by a general public, at least in Europe, that seems unable to appreciate the potential of their work. For the business leaders, the dreams are of successful companies. Some seek to shape benevolent corporations that will work towards reducing world hunger and disease. Many, however, are like Jacob and act out of self-interest. They primarily seek power for their organizations and control of the market. In this case "the market" may, in effect, be global human food supply. All these dreams interact and overlap at global, national and local levels.

Genetically modified crops

One of the most controversial aspects of modern technology concerns genetic modification, and particularly genetically modified (GM) crops. The well-known BBC radio and television interviewer John Humphrys began the chapter on GM in his book *The Great Food Gamble*[11] with two very different scenarios. In the first, the future is rosy, the world population is well fed by GM crops, and a whole host of beneficial medical interventions have become possible because of them. In the second scenario everything has gone wrong, genes have escaped from GM crops, new diseases are rife, and the large multinational agrichemical companies have gained complete control over the food chain. Humphrys' overall conclusion is that something closer to the second version of the future is more likely than the first, but is he right?

Advantages of GM crops

GM is simple in its basic concept. Desirable genes are snipped out of one organism and transferred to another with the aim of improving some characteristic of the latter. At present (2007), about 99% of all transgenic crops worldwide are either herbicide-resistant crops or Bt crops. Bt plants have been transformed to produce a natural insecticide from the bacterium, *Bacillus thuringiensis*, in their tissues. This makes the plants toxic or unpalatable to a whole range of insects. There is continuing development of GM crops, however, and the second generation will include plants that have been engineered to produce more vitamins, or contain more essential minerals such as iron.[12] The most famous of these is "golden rice". This has been produced by genetic engineering to make precursors of beta-carotene in the grain of rice, and these have a yellow colour as a result. Golden rice was developed to be used in areas where there is a shortage of vitamin A in the human diet. The original variety of golden rice was criticized, as a person would have to eat over 1.5 kg of the grain per day to gain enough vitamin A. By 2005, however, Golden Rice 2 had been produced and this contains 23 times more than the original. Golden rice has not yet been grown commercially, and has met much opposition, particularly from the anti-globalization lobby.

A third generation of GM crops is now being developed to produce medicines such as vaccines. In the longer term it may be possible to produce plants that are more able to deal with stressful environmental conditions, such as cold, extreme heat, drought or salinity. However, it is worth pointing out that those plants that are naturally found in such environments tend to grow very slowly, and have poor yields. I (Martin) worked on salinity resistance for my doctorate in the late 1970s and the idea of GM salt-tolerant crops was frequently discussed then. In 2007 there is still little sign of success. The problem with salt tolerance is that, unlike herbicide resistance, it is controlled by many genes, and is horrendously complex. It would be foolish to say that it can never be done, but I do begin to wonder.

Controversies over GM crops

GM crops cause a lot of arguments, but what are these about? The main ones are as follows:

1) Is there something intrinsically wrong with GM technology?

People that take this view worry that GM technology allows us to "play God". In other words they believe that it is not right to move genes from one organism to another, whatever the reason. Of course it is possible to argue that we were moving genes from one organism to another using conventional breeding techniques, long before the development of GM technology. Indeed, this was so, but in nearly all cases these were closely related organisms. Is it "right" to move scorpion genes into a plant? Or are there no boundaries at all to the types of manipulation that can be carried out? Donald Bruce, Don Horrocks and their colleagues13 wrote one of the most balanced books on GM from a Christian perspective and concluded that there was "little substantial biblical evidence to support an intrinsic objection to genetic engineering as such". Of course, many would disagree with this statement.

2) Is there a food safety risk?

For some this is still the most worrying potential problem, but the truth is that GM crops have now been grown in the United States for over ten years, and there have been no food problems at all.14 It is possible that any problems have a very long gestation period, but this seems increasingly unlikely. Of course, there is always the chance that a serious mistake will be made in the future, and that food safety will be compromised as a result of GM crops. That, however, is the risk we take with any technology.

3) Is there an environmental risk?

There are several potential environmental risks associated with GM crops.[15]

Some fear that the GM crop will harm non-target species. This might happen when an insect that is not a pest interacts with a plant that has been transformed to contain an insecticide. In general terms, this has not proved much of a problem, and, despite considerable concerns for species such as the Monarch butterfly in North America, there is little evidence of non-target organisms being badly affected.

People are concerned that the GM genes will escape to other organisms. This might happen when pollen from a GM plant fertilizes a related weed species or an organic crop of the same species. This has been shown to occur in oil seed rape where herbicide resistance genes have escaped to a related weed. The worry with this is that a "superweed" might be created that cannot be stopped by herbicides.

Could target organisms evolve herbicide resistance? For instance, weeds could become resistant to the herbicides applied to transgenic herbicide-tolerant crops. Herbicide-resistant weeds are already a major agricultural problem in conventional agriculture, and herbicide-resistant crops can encourage farmers to increase herbicide usage. Both the proponents and opponents of GM agree that these are the risks associated with the present generation of GM crops, and it seems that the latter two are most important.

4) Will multinational agrichemical companies get a stranglehold on the food chain?

It is funny, but many scientists I (Martin) mix with tend to think that the environmental activists are most concerned with 1–3 above, and particularly 2 (food safety). The environmental activists I mix with are concerned with 1–3 (particularly 3), but their bigger concern often tends to be the globalization aspects of GM. So often the scientists seek to reassure by explaining the science, but this can never address the activists' major worry.

Throughout the 1990s a few large multinational companies started to buy up seed companies and small cutting-edge biotechnology labs. They were so successful in doing this that GM crop technology is now largely controlled by a handful of multinationals. Thus, if the majority of crops grown in the world were GM, these companies would have power over them. It is possible that this control would be benevolent, but the evidence often suggests that the multinationals are more interested in profit than in "feeding the world". In the late 1990s, the agrichemical multinationals, which seemed to be invincible, had a considerable shock. The first, tentative, introduction of GM products onto supermarket shelves in the UK resulted in a consumer revolt, and they were rapidly withdrawn. Bruce and Horrocks, writing in 2001, commented, "the traditional sources of power in industry and government have been undermined by unexpected expression of consumer power, and the very astute campaigning of networks of environmentalists, consumer and development groups."[16] More shocks were to come.

The GM debate

In 2003 the UK government decided to hold a public consultation on GM crops and food.[17] They urged local organizations to hold public meetings at which the issues could be aired, and set up a special on-line questionnaire whereby the public were asked their views. We went along to the debate held in Dorchester Abbey, Oxfordshire on 3 July 2003. Eighty-three people were there, and they were overwhelmingly against GM.[18] One of the few who spoke in favour of GM was an organic farmer. Perhaps unwisely, he told the meeting that the only reason he was growing organic crops was that it increased his profit margins, and that he would switch to GM as soon as it was available! This goes some way towards debunking the idea that all organic farmers are "deep green".

The reasons given at the meeting for being anti-GM were various, but interestingly the main ones were concerns about globalization and the dominance of agrichemical companies. The overall results of the public consultation reflected those of the debate at Dorchester Abbey. There was widespread opposition to GM from the respondents, and it "highlighted a series of political issues, manifested in a strong and wide degree of suspicion about the motives, intentions and behaviour of those taking decisions about GM – especially government and multi-national companies".[19] Some pro-GM scientists and politicians claimed that the green lobby had hijacked the consultation, and that it did not truly reflect the views of the British public. Others tried to imply that the public did not properly understand the issues. If our sample of the public at Dorchester Abbey was anything to go by, however, they were very well informed on GM. Many cities, towns and councils went on to declare themselves "GM-free zones".[20] The truth is that the British public, for a whole variety of reasons, is highly suspicious of GM technology, particularly when it has to do with their crops and countryside.

Comparing attitudes to GM in the UK and the USA
It is interesting to ask why GM crops have been introduced so successfully and easily into the United States, when they have had such a tough time in the UK. There are several possible reasons:

• The big agrichemical companies tend to be based in the States and have local support there, whereas they lack that support in the UK.

• The trade justice movement in the UK is very strong indeed and this affects the attitude towards the multinational agrichemical companies.

• A number of food scares in the UK, particularly BSE and foot-and-mouth outbreaks, have made the British public very wary of science and scientists.

• One interesting observation is that there is a different perception of farmland in the two countries. In the USA much farming is conducted very intensively in specific areas, separated from wilderness areas. In the UK the British people regard the countryside as their area for recreation, and the idea of wandering through fields of "unnatural" GM crops is not very appealing.

• When large areas of the British countryside are in set aside or in stewardship schemes (see Chapter 8), are GM crops really needed or compatible?

Where are we on GM crops as we write in 2007? They are being grown in increasingly large amounts, and in increasing numbers of countries. It seems likely that it will not be long before the second-generation crops come on line. There are, however, many individuals and organizations that are implacably opposed, and some countries, like the UK, where there is little sign that GM crops will ever be grown. It will take considerable diplomacy to find a way forward that will allow for the advance of science and commercial success but also safeguard the interests of smaller companies, economically weaker nations and the biodiversity of the planet.

Rediscovering the mind of God

King Josiah had a vision for just government. His story focuses on the rediscovery of the Law during the renovation of the Temple in Jerusalem (2 Kings 22) and the impact of this discovery on the direction of the nation. We were reminded of this story recently when renovation work in an old library in Jesus College revealed a fragment of a printing plate hidden beneath floorboards.[21] It bore the text of Leviticus 19 from the King James Bible and may not have seen the light of day since the library was built in 1677. The passage is intriguing and as yet we can find no reason why it was hidden in this way. Leviticus 19 begins by encouraging us to imitate God's character: "Be holy because I, the LORD your God, am holy." Following God has never been just about seeking to keep to an external set of rules but about imitating him and seeking to be like him in the way we live our lives. This is what it really means to be made in the image of God. The question is: how can we be image-bearers?[22] The rest of the chapter outlines a series of guidelines. There are three groups of laws. Some concern the place of God in our lives, and these encourage us to worship him with sincerity and truth. Other laws are about integrity in our relationships with other people, and a third group encourages a sensitive treatment of nature. All three groups are interrelated.

The rediscovery of God's Law in King Josiah's day led to national repentance and revival, with a return to seeking to live according to the mind of God. Precepts such as those found in Leviticus 19 were re-established, bringing justice to the weaker in society as well as protecting nature. If the new resources of science and technology are to be used justly, there needs to be a commitment from governments and corporations that will guard against damaging self-interest. Likewise the global dimensions of many human and environmental problems, especially climate change, mean that we need governments to agree to act together to make sure the issues are addressed holistically for the good of all. The church is also an inter-national body and well placed to influence policies at this level. Our dream is similar to that of King Josiah. We wish to rediscover God's heart for his world and see this vision implemented at global and local levels. The three princi-ples outlined in Leviticus 19 provide a firm basis, as does the realization that they need addressing together. To achieve these goals practically there need to be both national and global agreements.

International environmental agreements and reports

At this point we will briefly outline some of the important international environmental agreements and reports that have been produced in the last 20 years. They form the background to much of this chapter and indeed to some material in previous chapters.[23] We have already had cause to mention the reports produced by the Intergovernmental Panel on Climate Change (IPCC)[24] in Chapter 3. The IPCC was formed by the World Meteorological Organisation and the United Nations Environment Programme in 1988. So far it has issued four reports, in 1990, 1995, 2001 and 2007, and these represent the authoritative scientific benchmark on climate change. Each report is compiled by hundreds of the world's top climate scientists.

In 1992 the Union of Concerned Scientists issued its "Warning to Humanity".[25] The signatories were 1,500 sci-entists, including Nobel Prize winners, and they warned that the global environment was in severe crisis. It is inter-esting that the atmosphere section mentions both ozone depletion and acid precipitation, but has nothing about carbon dioxide or global warming!! Times have changed. In the same year the Earth Summit (United Nations Conference on Environment and Development) was held in Rio de Janeiro, Brazil, and marked the beginnings of international action on climate change. The summit established the Framework Convention on Climate Change (FCCC), which aimed to stabilize greenhouse gases at levels that would not lead to dangerous climate change. To do this the FCCC set up the Kyoto Protocol, which was agreed in 1997. The aim of the protocol was to start to decrease the emissions of greenhouse gases. The initial aim was quite modest, and countries would be expected to decrease emissions by about 5% below 1990 levels by 2012. The protocol then had to be ratified by individual states, and it is here that it ran into problems. The United States, now led by George W. Bush, were firmly opposed. On 13 March 2001 he stated, "As you know, I oppose the Kyoto Protocol because it exempts 80 percent of the world, including major population centres such as China and India, from compliance, and would cause serious harm to the U.S. economy." The Bush opinion on climate change has gradually softened since this statement, but the USA never signed the Kyoto Protocol. After much international wrangling, however, the Kyoto Protocol came into force on 16 February 2005, the ninetieth day after 55 parties ratified. The negotiations are beginning to decide what replaces the Kyoto Protocol in 2012. As we have seen in Chapter 8, the UK government has already stated that it intends to cut emissions by 60% by 2050.

The final report that we will mention here is the Stern Review of 2006.[26] Although Sir Nicholas Stern's report was commissioned by the UK government, it undoubtedly had an international impact. While previous reports on climate change had been written mostly by scientists, Stern is a world-renowned economist, and provided a detailed economic analysis. The headline finding of the Stern Review was that the annual cost of stabilizing carbon dioxide in the atmosphere would be about 1% of world GDP, but the

cost of the damage from climate change if we did not stabilize CO_2 concentrations could be 10%.

International church initiatives

Against the background of mounting international concern
about the state of the global environment, and about climate change in particular, the international church bodies
have gradually swung into action. We have already seen in
Chapters 8 and 9 that national organizations and church
mission and development agencies have begun to take the
environment seriously. Here we will concentrate on international church statements. As long ago as 1990 the World
Convention in Seoul, Korea for "Justice, Peace and the
Integrity of Creation" made a covenant that included environmental commitments.[27] The covenant was taken forward in subsequent meetings of the World Council of
Churches, who continue to keep environmental concerns
as a priority. Seoul gave good practical guidelines, but left
some with a concern to clarify the theological position of
humans within creation.[28] In 1994, partly as a response to
the Rio Earth Summit and also responding to Seoul, came
the most influential statement from the evangelical
churches: "An Evangelical Declaration on the Care of
Creation".[29] The document was drafted by North American
theologians and scientists, including Cal DeWitt, Loren
Wilkinson and Ronald Sider. It emphasizes that the Earth
belongs to God and that humans are responsible as stewards of creation. Berry[30] provides a very detailed multi-
author commentary on the Declaration.

Many denominations have made statements on the
environment and these are gradually being followed up
with action. The worldwide Anglican communion has produced one of the best overall mission statements that we
are aware of in the Five Marks (or Strands) of Mission:[31]

1: To proclaim the good news of the kingdom

2: To teach, baptize and nurture new believers

3: To respond to human need by loving service

4: To seek to transform unjust structures of society

5: To strive to safeguard the integrity of creation and sustain and renew the life of the earth.

Every ten years the bishops of the Anglican Communion meet at Lambeth in London, UK. The first four "Marks" were adopted in the 1988 Lambeth Conference. The Fifth Mark was added in 1990 to take account of our call to the stewardship of creation.[32] This Mark is about "Seeing the Holy Spirit at work in the whole of creation, not just the bits of it we think we would like to be involved in".[33] Environment was not a strong focus at the 1998 Lambeth conference, which seemed to be dominated by the debate on human sexuality. However, there were two good resolutions on Creation and Ecology and since then many church leaders worldwide have engaged with "green" as a vital part of mission. In 2002 a group of Christians gathering for the Johannesburg summit held a pre-conference meeting, and decided to establish the Anglican Communion Environmental Network (ACEN)[34] to co-ordinate its work on an international scale. We predict that environment will feature strongly in Lambeth 2008.

Climate Forum 2002 and beyond

It is not very often that you attend an event only to discover much later that it was of historic importance, but that is what happened to us in July 2002. We were invited to attend Climate Forum 2002[35] in St Anne's College, Oxford University, and were there to represent A Rocha. The conference was jointly organized by the John Ray Initiative

(JRI)[36] from the UK and the Au Sable Institute for Environmental Studies[37] from the USA. The two prime movers behind Climate Forum 2002 were Sir John Houghton (JRI) and Professor Cal DeWitt (Au Sable). Their key idea was to bring over to the UK as many American Christian leaders as possible to convince them of the reality of climate change. Unfortunately for JRI and Au Sable, July 2002 was not that long after 11 September 2001, and that reduced the numbers coming. Nonetheless, over 70 church leaders and scientists from around the world came to the event, and we had some excellent presentations on both the science of climate change and the theology of creation care. There were a number of small group meetings at which the participants were asked to help produce a conference statement. The conference dinner was held in the hall of Jesus College, Sir John Houghton's college, and the former UK environment minister John Gummer gave the after dinner speech.

The conference statement concluded "We, the forum participants, recognize the urgency for addressing human induced climate change, repent of our inaction and commit ourselves to work diligently and creatively to adopt solutions in our own lives and in the communities we influence. We call upon leaders in churches, business and government to join us in recognizing human induced climate change as a moral and religious issue and to take necessary action to maintain the climate system as a remarkable provision in creation for sustaining all life on Earth." There was quite a flurry of activity after the conference while the final touches were put to the statement, and this was widely disseminated in church circles in both the UK and the USA. Then, however, all seemed to go quiet. The conference had a major impact on both of us, and from that time we found ourselves increasingly drawn into

JRI circles. But it looked as if it had failed with the States. We began to think that maybe it was just another conference, here today and gone tomorrow, and with no lasting influence. We were undoubtedly wrong to think that. In one of the conference small groups, Martin remembers a tall American pastor, Revd Richard Cizik, who made some very incisive comments. It turned out that Cizik, in his own words "had a conversion experience on the climate issue not unlike my conversion to Christ" at the conference in Oxford in 2002.[38] He went back to the States, sold his gas-guzzling RV (five miles per gallon) and bought a Toyota Prius, which is about ten times more efficient. This change in one man's personal lifestyle was a direct result of the Oxford conference, but it had a greater significance. Cizik was also a vice-president of the National Association of Evangelicals (NAE)[39] in the USA, an organization representing 30 million people, who attend 45,000 churches. From the time he returned to the States he started to lobby within his evangelical constituency. Cizik, a conservative Republican, wanted to convince as many of his compatriots as possible that caring for creation was a God-given duty, and that climate change was real.

In June 2004, NAE, the Evangelical Environmental Network and *Christianity Today* magazine sponsored a meeting at Sandy Cove in Maryland, USA for American evangelical leaders. Sir John Houghton was a keynote speaker, and at the end of the meeting the delegates committed themselves to discussing the issue of climate change with other leaders of the evangelical community. They aimed to produce a definitive statement on the issue, but were not ready to do so at that time, and instead made the Sandy Cove Covenant[40] while they consulted more widely. In the autumn of 2004, the NAE adopted "For the Health of the Nation: An Evangelical Call to Civic

Responsibility",[41] which included creation care as one of the organization's top seven priorities.

All the above activity led up to a statement in February 2006 by an alliance of 86 church leaders, the Evangelical Climate Initiative, entitled "Climate Change: An Evangelical Call to Action".[42] The main points of the statement show just how far opinion in the evangelical community in the States had shifted since the Oxford conference in 2002:

1: Human-induced climate change is real.

2: The consequences of climate change will be significant, and will hit the poor the hardest.

3: Christian moral convictions demand our response to the climate change problem.

4: The need to act now is urgent. Governments, businesses, churches and individuals all have a role to play in addressing climate change – starting now.

It is only fair to point out that not all in the American evangelical community agree with the above statement, and, in particular, Focus on the Family led by James Dobson have been very vocal opponents. There is no doubt now, however, that climate change is being debated by this community, and that this discussion will continue up to and beyond the next presidential election in 2008.

As a kind of a postscript to this story, in February 2007 another full-circle event happened for us. By this time Margot was chaplain of Jesus College, Oxford, and she was asked to lead a service in the chapel for BBC Sunday Worship on Radio 4 on the theme of "Creation held together in Christ",[43] timed to be broadcast live shortly after the IPCC 2007 report came out. Sir John Houghton was the preacher, and the service also featured a short recorded interview with Revd Richard Cizik.

The rich fool

One of the readings during our service on BBC radio was the parable of the rich fool (Luke 12:16–21). This man built bigger barns for his crops, thinking that he was secure and could enjoy anything that he wanted in life. But he was a fool because he had ignored God and that very night his life was demanded of him. There are many parallels between the rich fool and the attitude of some Western countries and multinational companies. Most, if not all, are using resources at an unsustainable level. From the security of comfortable offices, homes and recreational facilities, the environmental problems we face can seem distant. One day, however, we will be called to account, and very soon we will have to face the massive negative consequences of our overuse of resources. The next section of Luke is about sharing with others, and this is a major part of the practical mission of the church. It is as we refocus our lives away from materialism and towards caring for the poor and the Earth that we will find a way forward. This is the real dream that we need to work towards. The key is hope, and this will be the focus of our final chapter.

Hope and the resurrection of creation

Now faith is being sure of what we hope for and certain
of what we do not see.

Hebrews 11:1

Hope, the Earth and the Gospel

Almost every year since 1993 Sage has had a stand at the
Green Fair in Oxford (see photo 17). This is organized by
the Green Party, which is a significant force in local politics. The fair is always in early December and gives an
opportunity for finding exotic and unusual Christmas presents. We've mostly been the only Christian group present,
though certainly not the only spiritual one! One year, the
girl on the stand next to ours, offering palm reading, asked
if I (Margot) would mind it for a while so she could look
round the fair. I said I'd keep an eye on it but couldn't really
make any sales! When she returned she had tears in her
eyes. I asked her what was wrong. "There is no hope," she
said. "Everything is getting worse and worse and there is no
hope for our planet any more." I asked her if she knew we
were a Christian group and, when she said yes, I told her
that we had hope. From there I explained that God loved
his creation so much that he sent Jesus to die to redeem the
cosmos. Far from giving up on the world, God is holding it

together and will not let it fall into chaos. I was glad to see a glimmer of hope amid the tears and realized that my future gazing had given faith to a professional in the field!

The state of the planet

We've used this book to survey many of the environmental issues in our world and seen how they interconnect with our lives as humans and our faith as Christians. Sadly, many of the "issues" are actually problems, and it is easy to see why someone might feel without hope in the face of it all. Climate change is an overarching one but, as we have seen, there are many others, including biodiversity loss, soil erosion and water.[1] In the end it may turn out that human population is the biggest issue because it is driving climate change and exacerbating the other problems. When we consider the human suffering that is also a consequence of this misuse of the Earth, the situation does indeed look bleak. So why have hope?

Sir John Houghton quotes three reasons for hope.[2] Firstly, he is confident of the scientific community. Scientists from all parts of the world are committed to understanding the science behind global environmental problems and to finding solutions. Secondly, he believes that the technology is available to find a way forward. This will also mean that governments need to make the environment an issue high on their list of priorities. The most powerful nations will need to give a strong lead and exercise responsibility for tackling the global situation. We believe there are beginning to be signs that this is happening, and John's work with the American evangelicals, which we outlined in the previous chapter, is playing a part. There will need to be greater controls on multinational companies and more support for NGOs, but none of this is impossible, provided the will is there. The third reason for John's hope and ours is the firm belief that God is committed to his creation and that we do not have to struggle on our own. As we look to the future we believe as Christians that Christ himself holds the key to the salvation of our planet, and this will be the focus of our final chapter.

Held together in Christ

In Colossians, St Paul provides a cosmic understanding of Jesus as the one who holds all things together.

> [Christ] is the image of the invisible God, the firstborn over all creation. For by him all things were created: things in heaven and on earth, visible and invisible, whether thrones or powers or rulers or authorities; all things were created by him and for him. He is before all things, and in him all things hold together.
> (Colossians 1:15–17)

We have already considered the theme of interconnectedness in the Old Testament. It is also a strong idea within the environmental movement. Colossians provides a dynamic Christian understanding of this concept, firmly based on the belief that there is one God who is the creator of all. God could, in fact, be described as a "creating God", one who continues to be present in the universe and dynamically sustains all things as they continue to develop and change. This explains God's role in the past and present, but it does not end there; it points us to the future. The passage goes on to base Christ's supremacy over creation on his resurrection power. Paul teaches that, through his blood shed on the cross, God will bring about the ultimate reconciliation of the universe and make peace.[3] So there is a connection between creation, God's role in the world today and a hope for peace and reconciliation in the future. And at the heart of this is the resurrection. To understand this fully we will need to look at some of the texts on the future of the universe. As we turn to these, we will first consider some of the ways in which they have been misunderstood!

Trash the planet to speed the end?

In the early 1990s, I (Martin) was on sabbatical in Toronto, Canada. I had previously lived in Toronto when I was on a research contract there in 1987, and had adopted Stone Church[4] in the downtown area as my home church. So this was my church whenever I stayed there, and I went to both Sunday services and midweek meetings. It was excellent! At one evening meeting I got talking with a young man, and happened to mention that back in the UK I was involved in the Christian environmental movement. This was his response: "Jesus is coming back soon, and then we will have a new heaven and a new earth..." I guess if we know the book of Revelation we would have to agree with that. Then he went on to say, "So we don't have to worry about environmental issues..." I could not see the connection, but he followed this up with: "In fact, the quicker we mess up the planet, the quicker Jesus will return." Yikes! I had never come across this line of argument before, and was a bit stumped at the time.

The topic of eschatology, or the last days, or what happens at the end of time, is one of the most controversial for Christians. While some Christians seem to spend most of their time considering these matters, others hardly ever look at them, and some are very worried by the whole topic and adopt evasion tactics. There is little doubt, however, that just as ideas about how the Earth began influence how we think about the environment, so does what we think about its end.

I hope that, if you have read Chapters 1–10 of this book,

you will already have some answers for my friend in Toronto, but we need to spend a little time on this kind of thinking as versions of it are prevalent in some church circles around the world, and it does influence opinion even beyond the church.

A completely new heaven and Earth?

The key verse, Revelation 21:1, says, "Then I saw a new heaven and a new earth, for the first heaven and the first earth had passed away, and there was no longer any sea." Before we look in detail at what this verse actually means, let us assume for the moment that most of what I was told on that evening in Toronto was true. In this scenario, after the return of Jesus, the Earth is destroyed and God will create a totally new one. So what is the point in protecting the Earth? Margot often tells a story to answer this:

Imagine that your great-great-grandfather was a carpenter of great skill. Back in 1880 he spent six months of his life working on a wonderfully crafted rocking chair as a gift for his wife. This chair was then passed down through the family and now you are the proud owner. Of course you are aware that one day in the future the rocking chair will wear out, or it might be destroyed in a fire at your descendant's house. But does this mean that you do not look after the rocking chair as your most treasured heirloom? Of course you will care for it.

So even if the idea that God will destroy the Earth at the end of time and create a totally new one were correct, this does not mean that we should not protect what we presently have. That is taking the mindset of the worst of modern consumerism to its extreme religious conclusion. Certainly, suggesting that we can speed up the return of Jesus by destroying the planet just does not fit with biblical teaching. We should always be wary of any idea that we can do something to accelerate God's plans.

One might think that this "disposable paper plate" theology of the Earth is the preserve only of a few wacky individuals on the fringe of the church, and that this type of thinking has little influence. The idea might be fringe, but it certainly has a lot of influence. In 2005 it got an airing in the scientific journal, *Conservation Biology*, when David Orr wrote an article entitled "Armageddon versus Extinction", basically attacking Christians, and evangelical Christians in particular, for their views on eschatology.[5] Orr's article echoes that of Lynn White (see Chapter 5), but while White's main attack was based on Genesis, Orr concentrated on the other end of the Bible in Revelation. He argued that "belief in the imminence of the end times tends to make evangelicals careless stewards of our forests, soils, wildlife, air, water, seas and climate". Orr suggests that this kind of thinking has penetrated into many departments of the United States government, and has even been taken up by presidents, including Ronald Reagan and George W. Bush. Interestingly, Orr is almost as critical of his fellow conservation biologists, saying, "We seem tongue-tied when we consider the deeper questions about the causes and forces driving biotic impoverishment and climate change." He feels that conservation biologists are able to document our problems in great detail, but are completely unable to tackle reasons why humans are bringing them about.

Not too surprisingly Orr's article stirred up quite a hornets' nest, and there were two replies published in the same journal. One of these was written by an international group of Christians, all of whom are in conservation-related disciplines.[6] They criticized Orr on a number of grounds, including what they see as his misunderstanding of the natures of science and religion, his association of "evangelicals" with "right-wing conservatives", and his confrontational attitude. We will not go into these arguments here, but rather concentrate on what the authors had to say specifically about eschatology: "Evangelicals are not united in a belief that the universe as we know it will be destroyed at the end of time. Indeed, many believe that the overall thrust of biblical theology, built on a number of key texts such as Romans 8:19–23 and Colossians 1:15–20, is exactly the opposite." So maybe the "disposable paper plate" theology is not correct. Let us look at the evidence.

Waiting for liberation

The Romans passage is of course the famous "creation groaning" section, which we have already mentioned in Chapter 4. Romans 8:19–21 says, "The creation waits in eager expectation for the sons of God to be revealed. For the creation was subjected to frustration, not by its own choice, but by the will of the one who subjected it, in hope that the creation itself will be liberated from its bondage to decay and brought into the glorious freedom of the children of God." Most commentators suggest that it was God who subjected the creation to frustration when he cursed the Earth when Adam sinned. That was the past, but what will happen in the future? The fact that "the creation itself will be liberated from its bondage to decay" does not suggest that the creation will be totally destroyed. The Bishop of Durham, N.T. Wright, having surveyed the whole of the book of Romans, including Romans 8, concludes: "Paul's whole argument is that the renewal of God's covenant results in the renewal of God's creation."[7] If Wright is correct, we should expect a renewal of creation. How does this renewal happen? To understand this we need to return to Revelation 21:1.

New creation and new people

Scientists have many theories about the ultimate fate of the universe. Some predict that eventually gravity will overcome the expansion of the universe and it will implode inwards (the big crunch). Others see it expanding indefinitely and gradually ceasing to be the universe as we know it.[8] These ideas might seem to support the completely new Heaven and Earth concept, but they will actually help us to understand the manner of a continuing creation. First of all, we need to investigate the term "new" in Revelation 21:1. This uses the Greek word *kainos*, which is used in several other significant places in the Bible. Firstly, it is also used in Ephesians 4:24, where Christians are encouraged to leave behind their former ways of thinking and living and "put on the new (*kainos*) self, created to be like God in true righteousness and holiness". Clearly this does not mean that the original person is destroyed; rather it means that they are in some ways made new. The newness is in respect of quality rather than personhood. Secondly, in 2 Corinthians 5:17 it states: "Therefore, if anyone is in Christ, he is a new (*kainos*) creation." Again, the person will not be destroyed but will have a different quality of life. Romans 13:14 encourages us to "put on" Christ (AV), and this fits with the concept of being "in Christ" in 2 Corinthians. So what is this quality of newness and how is it focused on Christ?

Jesus destroyed death once and for all, through his death and resurrection. As humans made in God's image, when we come to Christ we are made new (*kainos*). His indwelling transforms our lives into an existence with him that has eternal dimensions. Our deaths lead to our resurrection and an eternal life with him. So it is death that is destroyed, not us. It is our real selves that are made new to live a life with Christ that has a different quality of being. So how can we use these ideas to understand what the terms "new Heaven and new Earth" actually mean?

Flood and destruction of the Earth

New Testament scholar Richard Bauckham draws an interesting parallel between the implication of Christ's death and resurrection for humans and for the whole of creation.[9] He believes that our present creation has an inbuilt tendency to "lapse back into nothing". This is because of the presence of death in creation and the forces of destruction. He explores the concept of chaos at creation and what it might mean for the future. This is an idea that God created the universe by holding back the forces of chaos. This force is a destructive potential within creation that could put it into reverse. Chaos is symbolized by dark waters of the deep. During the flood, these waters were released and rose up to destroy the inhabitants of the Earth. 2 Peter 3 draws on these ideas to explain what will happen at the end of the age. At first sight this looks like a destruction of the Earth, but it actually draws on the analogy of the flood, which purged rather than destroyed totally. What are destroyed are not Heaven and Earth but the dark forces within them. Revelation 20:14 describes these as death and Hades. Once these forces are removed, creation is "eternally secure from any threat of destructive evil".[10] The rainbow around the throne in Revelation 4:3 is a symbol of the covenant God made for the Earth at the time of Noah (Genesis 9:8–11). God promised that he would not again cut off all creatures and would never again destroy the Earth by flood. So what light does this shed on Revelation 21:1?

The Earth at the resurrection

The whole of the Bible is a story of God's faithfulness to his creation. As we reach the last chapters, we see that his faithfulness led him to the cross to conquer the forces of death and destruction that have been part of the dark side of creation and always present to spoil and destroy. At the resurrection these forces were overcome once and for all. At the culmination of time the forces of death in the universe will be destroyed once and for all. There will, in effect, be a resurrection of the universe as it is redeemed from these destructive forces and renewed in Christ. This new Heaven and Earth therefore, will not be a brand new Heaven and Earth unconnected to the ones we know. They will also not be a Heaven and Earth that become fixed and do not continue towards whatever is their ultimate cosmic destination. The ultimate fate of the universe as projected by physicists could still happen with this model because theologically what is described is a universe that has come through destruction and been brought to resurrection by God in an amazing creative and redeeming act of love. Our new Earth will lack the destructive powers that haunt it today and that is why there is no more sea (Revelation 21:1), because this is the symbol of those dark forces. But it does have us and it does have recognizable features of our present Earth. So we will now turn to look at what our resurrected Earth will be like.

The Earth, Isaiah and the Messianic age

Isaiah is one of my favourite books in the Bible and the Old Testament book most quoted in the New Testament. It has much to say on the environment, both in terms of how we should care for it today and also giving us a vision of the future Heaven and Earth. One of the most famous passages is chapter 11:1–9, which has the well-known image of the wolf living with the lamb. This is a picture of the Messianic age when peace on earth is finally established. It is an image of redeemed creation, but what leads up to it? In the first part of the chapter we are presented with a picture of a redeemer coming from the "stump of Jesse". Christians frequently associate this with the birth of Christ because of the reference to the house of David (son of Jesse), but it can more naturally be applied to a post-resurrection Jesus. Verse 1 "A shoot will come up from the stump of Jesse", speaks of new life coming out of death, and verses 3-5 speak of a redeemer coming to judge the world.

If these are references to the second coming of the resurrected Christ, then the famous passage about a redeemed and harmonious creation is also a resurrection passage. In this renewed creation we find wild and domestic animals living in harmony with one another and with humans. They have a sense of peace about them that speaks of a very different world from our own. Similarly, the beautiful passage in Isaiah 35 speaks of a redeemed creation where the glory of the Lord brings healing and abundant fruitfulness. A land that is parched becomes a source of springs and a place of the redeemed. Isaiah 11 is quoted in Isaiah 65:17–25. This is the first place where the term "new Heaven and Earth" is used in the Bible. It provides a picture of peace, prosperity and long life. Disease will be a thing of the past, wild animals will be tamed and live in harmony with domesticated ones, and humans will plant vineyards and enjoy their homes. The city of Jerusalem will be part of this new age and will be a delight.

All these images are only glimpses of this new world but it provides an image of harmony between God, people and the rest of creation, in which humans are working as stewards of the earth (planting and domesticating). It is an image of abundant blessing and joy. It is not surprising that St John was inspired by this image to describe the future at the end of Revelation.

The Earth, revelation and the water of life

Revelation 21 and 22 announce the new Heaven and Earth and the end to death and destruction. The description is not, however, of a wild place of outstanding natural beauty, but of an urban image of the New Jerusalem. This ties in with Isaiah's vision which also focused on Jerusalem and its surrounds. But it does not lack natural features, and if we look at these more closely we can see why Jerusalem is the focus and why it is at the heart of a redeemed creation. Jerusalem itself is both the place of the people of God and the place where God's glory dwells. It is, therefore, the fulfilment of the restored relationship between God and humanity. The symbolism used is that of a bride with her bridegroom.

In chapter 22 we find the river of life flowing from the throne of God, down the middle of the main street of the city (see photo 32). This draws on the vision in Ezekiel 47 where the river flows out of the city, through the desert and into the sea. The desert is made fruitful and the sea is made fresh. This is a wonderful miracle of redemption and healing. Jerusalem was historically a city that struggled to find a secure source of fresh water. The town was served by the spring of Gihon that lay outside the city. This always made it vulnerable to attack and there were a number of attempts to secure the source by digging tunnels and pools (there is still a famous tunnel built by King Hezekiah that the more intrepid visitor to Jerusalem can walk through). These in turn became weak points of the city, and David's men managed to conquer Jerusalem by climbing up the water shaft (2 Samuel 5:8). Now, in the new creation, the city that had always struggled to gain water will become the source of the Water of Life (22:1). Furthermore, the city that had been vulnerable and was so heavily defended will become a redeemed city with open gates. The nations freely go up to it and bring their glory and honour. It is therefore the culmination of redemption resulting in the restored relationship between humans and God. This is intimately connected with the River of Life and restored relationships with the rest of creation. On the banks of the river is the Tree of Life, producing fruit every month and leaves that are for the healing of the nations. So we find the complete healing of the three-way relationship between God, people and planet. All are brought into harmony and the source of this is the city. Beautifully, nature (in the form of the leaves and the water) is the source of healing for humanity, and the city (as the source of the River of Life) is the source of healing for nature in the blossoming of the desert and the transformation of the sea in the prophecies of Isaiah and Ezekiel.

So our resurrected Earth will be blessed by God, who will be tangibly present (see photo 33). It will have harmonious relationships between God, people and the rest of nature. It will be a place where human stewardship is worked out and nature is harmonized through human creativity. As we leave this vision and turn back to our own lives, we should be both assured and challenged. As the people of God, we are charged to be bearers of the first fruits of this new creation within our own far from perfect world. In our book we have looked at the many ways in which we can do that, but it should not just be about making practical changes with a vague feeling that caring for the planet is a biblical thing to do. We should do every action (whether spiritual, intellectual or practical) as an action that reveals God's kingdom on Earth and proclaims his reign and redemption to come. As Christian communities we are scattered among the nations. Our kingdom is one that can bring these nations healing.

City of gold

There is a traditional children's hymn that says of the Bible, "It begins with a tale of a garden, and ends with the city of gold".[11] We began our book just over a year ago on the shores of Connemara in Ireland. We are ending in Brussels, Belgium, where we are having a short holiday after a long summer of writing! It is an attractive city, though when we arrived on the Eurostar it did not look much like the New Jerusalem described above. It is, however, a city of gold. Brussels, along with Washington, Beijing, London and others, is one of the seats of power where decisions are made that will make or break our planet. Neither of us had ever been to Brussels before, and we decided on the train from Waterloo,[12] London that we would take a holiday but also look for the signs of the hope that is the theme of this chapter.

In many respects the Eurostar trains[13] are themselves a sign of hope. The Channel Tunnel was a project built by visionaries who wanted to speed up travel between the UK and the continent. The project was commenced in 1987, and it was officially opened in 1994. It has been beset by financial problems at times, but the fact that it exists is a testament to co-operation between governments, the skill of engineers, and the foresight of the business community. None of these could have predicted in the 1980s that carbon emissions would become such an issue in the early part of the 21st century. It is now possible to travel from London to Brussels or Paris in almost the same time as flying (if you take into account the large amount of time spent at airports checking in, taxiing on runways, and retrieving your baggage afterwards), but with greatly reduced carbon emissions. Not surprisingly, Eurostar are promoting their trains as a green option, and outside

Waterloo Station we saw an advertisement hoarding on which they were claiming that they used only one-tenth of the carbon that a flight does.[14]

On arrival in Brussels, we soon discovered that the city has a highly developed public transport system, with fast and efficient underground trains linked to trams and buses. The Brussels authorities evidently had the prudence not to scrap their trams, as happened in many British cities from the 1930s to the 1960s. To get to the underground trains we used escalators. Walking towards one on the first day in Brussels, we noticed it was not moving, and assumed it was not working. Then it suddenly switched on as we passed a sensor and walked on. It is quite a simple energy-saving device, and we wondered why escalators in other countries do not have it.

The weekend we were visiting just happened to be that of the annual beer festival, which took place in the *Grand-Place* (Market Square). We sampled Kwak, which is served in a mini-yard of ale supported by a wooden retort stand. Beer is of course a very serious business in Belgium. We were pleased to see that it has also become an environmentally aware business, as one of the poster boards in the *Grand-Place* gave details of recycling percentages for bottles and cans.

As is our custom, we sought out the National Botanic Garden of Belgium[15] at Meise, just north of Brussels. We spent a pleasant day wandering around the sections that were open to the public. In the greenhouses the displays of economic plants showed an understanding of Third World issues that would not have been seen in the past in this type of context. Much of the work of the scientists at the botanic gardens of the world goes on out of the public gaze. This is the case at Meise, where the emphasis is on the conservation of plants from Belgium and Africa.

We also make a point of visiting a local church whenever we are abroad on a Sunday. Margot asked a friend before we went to Brussels, and he suggested Holy Trinity, which was a conveniently short walk from our hotel.[16] There are times when one feels that the Holy Spirit has planned things well in advance, and our visit to Holy Trinity was certainly one of them. Imagine our surprise when we opened the church newsletter for that week to find that the church council had just decided to do an environmental audit of the church, using Eco-Congregation[17] material! The morning service of baptism and communion included a reading of the Noah passage mentioned above (Genesis 9:8–11). The preacher, Robert Innes, connected the covenant God made with Noah with the modern day issues of climate change and sea-level rise. We could not resist returning for the evening service on creation (Genesis 1). The day seemed to have been designed for us. It was, in many ways, a confirmation that we were on the right track with this book. But, more than that; it was a clear sign that the church was waking up to its environmental responsibilities. Hope.

On our final day in Brussels we decided to take a walk from Tervuren,[18] south-east of the city, through some wonderful beech forests and around the lakes, looking at the birds. Towards the end of the walk we visited the Royal Museum for Central Africa.[19] The most interesting section for us was the newly constructed history of Belgium's colonial involvement in the Congo. The displays were very critical of the colonial rule that ended in 1960, but had little to offer in the way of hope for today. After the Belgians left, the country fell into turmoil, and a series of wars left the Congo in a mess. In 2006, Congo had its first democratic elections for 46 years, and although fighting continues in some parts of the country these were a small glimmer of hope. As we have seen throughout this book, the developing world, and Africa in particular, is the area most affected by environmental degradation, and is the most likely to suffer from climate change in the future.

Our week in Brussels did give us many reasons for hope. We saw examples of actions being taken for the benefit of the environment at individual, community, national and international levels. All kinds of people were involved: scientists, engineers, business people, politicians, churchgoers, and lots more. A tremendous shift in thinking is taking place, though, undoubtedly, the needs of the developing world offer the greatest challenge for us all.

Moving forward, inspired by faith

The letter to the Hebrews in the New Testament was written to inspire faith. It begins with an amazing passage about Jesus, who is heir to all things and through whom God made the universe. Jesus is the radiance of God's glory and holds all things together though his word (Hebrews 1:2–3). The cosmic vision of the writer of this book echoes that of St Paul in Colossians 1:15–17. Both see Christ as the one who holds the universe and ultimately will not let it fall apart (see photo 34). Our small signs of hope can seem but a drop in the ocean compared to the size of the environmental challenge that we are faced with this century. We seem literally light years away from the vision of Isaiah and Revelation 21–22, and may even feel that this century has more in common with the earlier chapters of Revelation, when plagues and disasters were being poured out upon the Earth at a terrifying rate.

The writer to the Hebrews does not just leave us with the cosmic vision, however. He earths his ideas in some very practical teaching about faith. In chapter 11 he begins by placing our faith on the foundation of trusting in God's power as creator. He then gives us a fast-forwarded view of the Old Testament with all the characters who had faith and who worked to see God's kingdom become a reality on Earth. None of them saw the fulfilment of their vision, and yet all of them played an essential part in bringing it to reality. This century, none of us will see the full outcome that can be achieved through changing our lifestyles and working towards a more just and sustainable world. If we have faith, however, we should take inspiration from those who have gone before us and know that our efforts will be a part of building Christ's kingdom and that he will be alongside us as he holds together the very fabric of our world.

There may be many things that will hold us back. We might so fear the future that we try to avoid thinking about it. We might resort to a false pragmatism of setting aside environmental goals to achieve more "spiritual" or humanitarian ones. But, if we take up the environmental challenge, we will find it is the vital missing element in the work of Christ's kingdom. Hebrews 12 begins, "Therefore, since we are surrounded by such a great cloud of witnesses, let us throw off everything that hinders and the sin that so easily entangles, and let us run with perseverance the race marked out for us. Let us fix our eyes on Jesus the author and perfecter of our faith." As we focus on Jesus, we find our sights set on one who owned very little, cared for the poor, conquered death and offers us hope for the future as we trust in him. Christian hope is not a false optimism that closes its eyes and hopes for the best. It is realistic about the pain and challenges of the world, and firm in its belief in the strength of God to meet those challenges and be with us as we face them.

Jesus said:

> You did not choose me, but I chose you and appointed you to go and bear fruit – fruit that will last. Then the Father will give you whatever you ask in my name. This is my command: Love each other. (John 15:16–17)

Notes

Chapter 1: A living planet made for God's glory
1. Shirihai, H. (1996) *Birds of Israel*, London: Academic Press, p. 338. Pied kingfishers (*Ceryle rudis*) are quite common in Northern Israel, particularly around the Sea of Galilee. Their distinctive black and white colouring is unlike that of most other kingfishers.

2. For a practical account of the different ethical approaches to the environment, see Attfield, R. (2003) *Environmental Ethics*, Cambridge: Polity Press.

3. Wright, C.J.H. (1983) *Living as the People of God*, Leicester: IVP, p. 19.

4. For a more detailed but very readable account, see Redfern, M. (2003) *The Earth. A Very Short Introduction*, Oxford: Oxford University Press.

5. See Williams, R.J.P. and Frausto da Silva, J.J.R. (2006) *The Chemistry of Evolution. The Development of our Ecosystem*, Amsterdam: Elsevier. This book gives a comprehensive account of the chemistry of life processes. The section on p. 7 considers the atmosphere of the planets and the importance of water for life.

6. For a good introduction to soils, see Ashman, M.R. and Puri, G. (2002) *Essential Soil Science*, Oxford: Blackwell.

7. Wikipedia has very good coverage of tsunamis, and the Boxing Day 2004 event in particular. See http://en.wikipedia.org/wiki/Tsunami

8. These figures are based on the US geological survey of 1967.

9. See 'The comprehensive assessment of water management in agriculture' (2006), International Water Management Institute (IWMI), Colombo, Sri Lanka: www.iwmi.cgiar.org/assessment

10. For a detailed account of the hydrological cycle, see Park, C.

(2001) *The Environment. Principles and Applications*, 2nd edn, London: Routledge.

11. See Park (2001), p. 479.

12. See http://en.wikipedia.org/wiki/The_Day_After_Tomorrow for details of the film and critiques of the science behind it.

13. See Williams, R.J.P. and Frausto da Silva, J.J.R. (2006), p. 90, for the detailed chemistry of the ozone layer.

14. See Park (2001), p. 271.

Chapter 2: Partners with God for a living planet
1. Ray, J. (1691) *The Wisdom of God manifested in the Works of Creation*. This book and much more about John Ray can be downloaded from the John Ray Initiative web site. See: http://www.jri.org.uk/ray/wisdom/index.htm

2. Even with plantation wood, care needs to be taken. Plantations themselves can endanger species. One species of shorea (a tree similar to teak, used for park benches) is under threat because it grows only in one locality that has been turned into a plantation. This species (*Shorea kuantanensis*) is described as critically endangered in 'The World List of Threatened Trees'. See Oldfield, S. (2001) Rediscovering and conserving endangered trees. *Oryx* **35**, 170–171.

3. This extract was first published by Margot Hodson as an *Eco-column* in *The Door*, Diocese of Oxford Newspaper, September 2005.

4. Barr, J. (1972) The ecological controversy and the Old Testament. *Bulletin of the John Rylands Library* **55**, 9–22.

5. DeWitt, C.B. (1995) Ecology and ethics: Relation of religious belief to ecological practice in the Biblical tradition. *Biodiversity and Conservation* **4**, 838–848.

6. Gaston, K.J. and Spicer, J.I. (2004) *Biodiversity. An Introduction*, Oxford: Blackwell Publishing.

7. Gaston and Spicer (2004), p. 2.

8. These are: Australia, Brazil, China, Colombia, Congo, Ecuador,

India, Indonesia, Madagascar, Malaysia, Mexico, Papua New Guinea, Peru, Philippines, South Africa, United States and Venezuela.

9. Gaston and Spicer (2004), p. 63.

10. Myers, N., Mittermeier, R.A., Mittermeier, C.G., Da Fonseca, G.A.B. and Kent, J. (2000) Biodiversity hotspots for conservation priorities. *Nature* **403**, 853–858.

11. The National Botanic Gardens at Glasnevin in Dublin: www.botanicgardens.ie

12. For more on the Wollemi Pine, see www.wollemipine.com

13. See Millennium Ecosystem Assessment (2005) Ecosystems and Human Well-being: Biodiversity Synthesis. World Resources Institute, Washington, DC, p. 17. Published on-line at www.millen-niumassessment.org

14. France, P. (1986) *An Encyclopaedia of Bible Animals*, Beckenham, UK: Surry Hills, Australia: Croom Helm Publishers.

15. Hodson, M.R. (2000) *A Feast of Seasons*, London: Monarch.

16. Katz, E. (ed.) (1992) *A New Classified Concordance of the Bible: A Hebrew-English Thesaurus of the Bible,* Jerusalem: Kiryat Sefer.

17. Olley, J.W. (2001) The wolf the lamb and the little child. Transforming the diverse Earth community in Isaiah. In N.C. Habel and S. Wurst (eds) *The Earth Story in the Psalms and the Prophets. The Earth Bible*, Vol.4, Sheffield: Sheffield Academic Press, pp. 219-229.

18. Nick Collinson is now Head of Conservation Policy at the Woodland Trust – www.woodland-trust.org.uk

19. Now Pond Conservation – www.pondconservation.org.uk

20. These are animals without a backbone that can be seen with the naked eye. If you want the full list, the pond macroinverte-brates are beetles, flatworms, leeches, snails, shrimps, mayflies, stoneflies, dragonflies, water bugs, alderflies and caddis flies.

21. A subsequent record for Ebernoe Common, West Sussex in 1999 cannot be confirmed because the specimen has been lost.

22. Collinson, N.H., Biggs, J., Corfield, A., Hodson, M.J., Walker, D., Whitfield, M. and Williams, P.J. (1995) Temporary and permanent ponds: An assessment of the effects of drying out on the conservation value of aquatic macroinvertebrate communities. *Biological Conservation* **74**, 125–133.

23. For a clear and relatively simple account of the aquatic and terrestrial biomes of the world, see Campbell, N.A., Reece, J.B. and Mitchell, L.G. (1999) *Biology*, 5th edn, Menlo Park, California: Addison Wesley, pp. 1034–1043.

24. Hareuveni, N. (1980) *Nature in our Biblical heritage*, Israel: Neot Kedumim.

25. "Maquis" is the Mediterranean type of chaparral. There is a similar type of vegetation in California and elsewhere, but made up of different species.

26. Hepper, F.N. (1992) *The Illustrated Encyclopaedia of Bible Plants*, Leicester: Inter-Varsity Press.

27. Shirihai, H. (1996) *Birds of Israel*, London: Academic Press, p. 335.

28. Shirihai (1996), p. 303.

29. Carson, R. (1962) *Silent Spring*, Houghton Mifflin.

30. Schwartz, E. (2002) Mystery and stewardship, wonder and connectedness. In H. Tirosh-Samuelson (ed.) *Judaism and Ecology, Created World and Revealed World*, Cambridge, MA: Harvard CSWR, p. 94.

Chapter 3: Pushing the planet into free fall

1. Sir John Houghton. *The Guardian*, Monday 28 July 2003.

2. See Winterhalder, K. (1984) Environmental degradation and rehabilitation in the Sudbury area. Northern Ontario: Environmental perspectives. *Laurentian University Review* **16** (2), 15–47. And Gunn, J., Keller, W., Negusanti, J., Potvin, R., Beckett, P. and Winterhalder, K. (1995) Ecosystem recovery after emission reductions: Sudbury, Canada. *Water, Air, and Soil Pollution* **85**, 1783–1788.

3. Kidner, D. (1981) *The Message of Hosea*, Leicester: IVP, p. 46.

4. Andersen F.I. and Freedman D.N. (1980) Hosea: A new translation with introduction and commentary. *The Anchor Bible*, Vol. 24. New York: Doubleday and Company, Inc.

5. For details of the Convention on Long-range Transboundary Air Pollution, see www.unece.org/env/lrtap/

6. Sliggers, J. and Kakebeeke, W. (2004) *Clearing the Air. 25 years of the Convention on Long-range Transboundary Air Pollution*, New York and Geneva: United Nations.

7. Dr Andy Gosler is Human Sciences Lecturer in Biological Conservation at Oxford University and churchwarden at Holy Trinity, Headington Quarry.

8. Gosler, A.G, Higham, J.P. and Reynolds, S.J (2005). Why are birds' eggs speckled? *Ecology Letters* **8**, 1105–1113.

9. Gosler, A.G. et al. (2005)

10. Snails require calcium to produce their shells.

11. Wenham, G.J. (1987) *Word Biblical Commentary, Volume 1, Genesis 1–15*. Dallas, Texas: Word incorporated.

12. Isaac Abravanel was a famous philosopher and biblical commentator who lived from 1437–1508 in Portugal, Spain and Italy. This reference is in Leibowitz, N. (1972) *Studies in Bereshit, Genesis*, Jerusalem: The Jewish Agency, p. 17.

13. Leibowitz (1972).

14. Ellul, J. (1972) *The Meaning of the City*, Grand Rapids, Michigan: W.B. Eerdmans, pp. 2–5.

15. Cassuto, U. (1961) *A Commentary on the Book of Genesis, Part 1: From Adam to Noah*. First published in Hebrew in 1944, English translation by I. Abrahams, Jerusalem: Magnus Press.

16. Mannion, A.M. (1995) *Agriculture and Environmental Change*, Chichester: John Wiley and Sons.

17. For a short account of climate change, see Maslin, M. (2004) *Global Warming. A Very Short Introduction*, Oxford: Oxford

University Press. For a more detailed account, see Houghton, J. (2004) *Global Warming. The Complete Briefing*, 3rd edn, Cambridge: Cambridge University Press.

18. See www.wmo.ch

19. The Intergovernmental Panel on Climate Change (IPCC) publishes many reports on this topic, and they are available at www.ipcc.ch

20. See http://en.wikipedia.org/wiki/Hurricane_Katrina for details of Hurricane Katrina.

21. For two very different books on the Christian response to climate change and its effects, see: McDonagh, S. (2006) *Climate Change. The Challenge to Us All*, Dublin: Columba, and Spencer, N. and White, R. (2007) *Christianity, Climate Change and Sustainable Living*, London: SPCK.

22. Oreskes, N. (2004) The scientific consensus on climate change. *Science* **306**, 1686.

23. The website of the film is at www.climatecrisis.net For details of the controversy surrounding the film, see http://en.wikipedia.org/wiki/An_Inconvenient_Truth. The book is Gore, A. (2006) *An Inconvenient Truth: The Planetary Emergency of Global Warming and What We Can Do About It*, Emmaus, USA: Rodale Books.

24. Marshall, E. (2006) Royal Society takes a shot at ExxonMobil. *Science* **313**, 1871.

25. The Royal Society (2007) *Climate Change Controversies. A Simple Guide,* London: Royal Society. This is also available at: www.royal-soc.ac.uk/page.asp?id=6229

Chapter 4: Standing room only for the creatures of the Earth

1. Prance, G. (1996) *The Earth under Threat. A Christian Perspective*, Glasgow: Wild Goose Publications.

2. Livi-Bacci, M. (2001) *A Concise History of World Population*, 3rd edn. Oxford: Blackwell. pp. 24–28.

3. Livi-Bacci (2001).

4. Heilig G.K. (1994) How many people can be fed on earth? In W. Lutz (ed.) *The Future Population of the World. What Can We Assume Today?* London: Earthscan Publications Ltd, pp. 207–261.

5. Livi-Bacci (2001), p. 192.

6. Frejka T. (1994) Long-range global population projections. In W. Lutz (ed.) *The Future Population of the World. What Can We Assume Today?* London: Earthscan Publications Ltd, pp. 3–15.

7. Clarke, J.I. (2002) The growing concentration of world population from 1950 to 2050. In H. Macbeth and P. Collinson (eds) *Human Population Dynamics. Cross-disciplinary Perspectives*, Cambridge: Cambridge University Press, pp. 41–64.

8. The state of food insecurity in the world 2003 (SOFI 2003). Food and Agriculture Organization of the UN (FAO).

9. Mannion, A.M. (1995) *Agriculture and Environmental Change*, Chichester: John Wiley.

10. See the BBC website – Chinese challenge one child policy. (25 May 2007). http://news.bbc.co.uk/1/hi/world/asia-pacific/6694135.stm

11. Ding, Q.J. and Hesketh, T. (2006) Family size, fertility preferences, and sex ratio in China in the era of the one child family policy: Results from national family planning and reproductive health survey. *British Medical Journal* **333**, 371–373.

12. Leibowitz, N. (1972) *Studies in Bereshit, Genesis,* Jerusalem: The Jewish Agency.

13. Guillebaud, J. (2000) Population numbers and environmental degradation. In R.J. Berry (ed.) *The Care of Creation*, Leicester: Inter-Varsity Press, pp. 155–160.

14. Dr Mike Pepler initially trained in electronic engineering, completing his PhD in 2000, but after helping found PowerSwitch in 2004 he retrained in renewable energy and now works as a consultant for a charity promoting local sustainable energy. See www.powerswitch.org.uk

15. Association for the study of Peak Oil and gas (ASPO): www.peakoil.net

16. EIA: http://tonto.eia.doe.gov/dnav/pet/hist/mcrfpus2a.htm

17. Petroleum Week (16 March 1956)
www.hubbertpeak.com/hubbert/ProductionCrisis.pdf

18. DTI: www.dtistats.net/energystats/dukes06.pdf pp. 265–266.

19. Energy Bulletin: www.energybulletin.net/primer.php

20. Kerr, R.A. (2007) Even oil optimists expect energy demand to outstrip supply. *Science* **317**, 437.

21. See Millennium Ecosystem Assessment (2005) Ecosystems and human well-being: Biodiversity synthesis. Washington, DC: World Resources Institute, p. 18. Published on-line at www.millenniu-massessment.org

22. World Resources Institute: www.wri.org

23. World Resources Institute.

24. Wright, S.J. (2005) Tropical forests in a changing environment. *Trends in Ecology and Evolution* **20**, 553–560.

25. Lewis, S.L. (2006) Tropical forests and the changing earth system. *Philosophical Transactions of the Royal Society, Series B* **361**, 195–210.

26. The Environment Agency – www.environment-agency.gov.uk

27. Morris, P. and Therivel, R. (eds) (2001) *Methods of Environmental Impact Assessment*, 2nd edn, London: Spon Press.

28. Keilman, N. (2003) The threat of small households. *Nature* **421**, 489–490.

29. Jermy, A.C., Long, D., Sands, M.J.S., Stork, N.E. and Winser, S. (1995) *Biodiversity Assessment: A Guide to Good Practice*, London: Department of the Environment/HMSO.

30. Sale, J. (2000) Biodiversity loss. JRI Briefing Paper No. 4. Available at www.jri.org.uk/brief/biodiversity.htm

31. Conservation International – www.conservation.org

32. See Chapter 2 for the story of the Wollemi Pine, another recently-discovered large organism.

33. Groombridge, B. and Jenkins, M.D. (2000) *Global Biodiversity: Earth's Living Resources in the 21st Century*, Cambridge, UK: World Conservation Press.

34. Haberl, H., Wackernagel, M., and Wrbka, T. (2004) Land use and sustainability indicators. An introduction. *Land Use Policy* **21**, 193–198.

35. Dr Andy Gosler is Human Sciences Lecturer in Biological Conservation at Oxford University and churchwarden at Holy Trinity, Headington Quarry.

36. The essential references for climate change and great tit nesting are: McCleery, R. H. and Perrins, C. M. (1998) Temperature and egg-laying trends, *Nature* **391**, 30–31; and Cresswell, W. and McCleery, R. (2003) How great tits maintain synchronization of their hatch date with food supply in response to long-term variability in temperature, *Journal of Animal Ecology* **72**, 356–366.

37. See, for example, Bradley, I. (1990) *God is Green,* London: Darton, Longman and Todd.

38. Meyer, P.W. (1988) Commentary on Romans. In Mays, J. L. (ed.) *Harper's Bible Commentary*, The Society of Biblical Literature, San Francisco: Harper and Row.

39. GEO-4 Global Environmental Outlook: environment for development (2007) United Nations Environment Programme (UNEP). See www.unep.org/geo/geo4/media/index.asp

Chapter 5: The seeds of history

1. Goodstein, L. (2005) Evangelical leaders swing influence behind effort to combat global warming. *The New York Times*, 10 March, 2005.

2. Chadwick, H. (2001) *Augustine: A Very Short Introduction*, Oxford: Oxford Paperbacks.

3. Seasoltz, R. (2005) Benedictines. In: L. Jones (ed.) *Encyclopaedia of Religion*, Vol. 2, 2nd edn, Detroit: Macmillan Reference USA, pp. 821–822. (15 vols.)

4. These Eastern churches are a complex group of different denominations. The most widely known are the Russian and Greek

Orthodox, who broke away from the Western (Roman Catholic) Church in the 11th century.

5. See, for example, the work of Rowan Williams for more on this perspective of the Trinity: Williams, R. (ed.) (1999) *Sergei Bulgakov: Towards a Russian Political Theology*, Edinburgh: T. & T. Clark.

6. For a good introduction to Eastern approaches to the environment, see Keselopoulos, A.G. (2001) *Man and the Environment*, Crestwood, NY: St Vladimir's Seminary Press.

7. For example, the Celtic church followed the Eastern tradition of dating Easter according to Passover, rather than by the vernal equinox, as practised by Rome.

8. Simpson, R. (1995) *Exploring Celtic Spirituality*, London: Hodder and Stoughton.

9. Rees, N. (1992) *St David of Dewisland: Patron Saint of Wales*, Llandysul, Ceredigion: Gomer Press.

10. Martin, B. (2004) Lord of lark and lightning: Reassessing Celtic Christianity's ecological emphases. *Journal of Religion and Society* **6**, http://moses.creighton.edu/JRS/2004/2004-11.html

11. Maimonides, M. (2004) *The Guide for the Perplexed* (translated from the original [1190]. Arabic text by M. Friedlander [1881], with an introduction by D. Taffel). New York: Barnes and Noble, p. 462.

12. Maimonides (2004) p. 461.

13. Bauckham, R. (2006) Modern domination of nature – Historical origins and biblical critique. In R.J. Berry (ed.) *Environmental Stewardship*, London: T.& T. Clark.

14. White, L. (1967) The historical roots of our ecological crisis. *Science* **155**, 1203–1207.

15. Ruddiman, W.F. and Thomson, J.S. (2001) The case for human causes of increased atmospheric CH_4 over the last 5,000 years. *Quaternary Science Reviews* **20**, 1769–1777.

16. Ruddiman, W. (2003) The anthropogenic greenhouse era began thousands of years ago. *Climatic Change* **61**, 261–293.

17. Mason, B. (2004) The hot hand of history. *Nature* **427**, 582–583.

18. This was later developed by Linnaeus (1707–1778) into the binomial system of classification that is still used today.

19. Russell, C. (1995) *Cross-currents. Interactions between Science and Faith*, London: Christian Impact.

20. Russell (1995).

21. James Usher (1581–1656) calculated that the world began in 4004 BC.

22. Isaiah 24:5.

23. White, L. (1967) The historical roots of our ecological crisis. *Science* **155**, 1203–1207.

24. Næss, A. (2005) The basics of Deep Ecology. The Trumpeter Journal of Ecosophy. Volume 21, Number 1 (2005) ISSN: 0832-6193 (This paper is a revised version of one given in a lecture in Canberra, Australia, in 1986).

25. Lovelock, J. E. (1972) Gaia as seen through the atmosphere. *Atmospheric Environment* **6**, 579–580.

26. See Dammers, H. (1982) *A Christian Lifestyle: A Parable of Sharing*, London: Hodder and Stoughton. For more recent material, see www.lifestyle-movement.org.uk

27. See www.christian-ecology.org.uk For more details, see Chapter 8.

28. Sider, R. J. (1990) *Rich Christians in an Age of Hunger* (3rd edn), Downers Grove, IL: Inter-Varsity Press. First published in 1977, this remains one of the most important books on this topic.

29. See Chapter 9 for more details.

30. See Chapter 9 for more details: www.tearfund.org

31. See http://en.arocha.org/home/

32. See Chapter 10 for more details.

33. See www.jri.org.uk

34. See Chapter 10 for more on the work of JRI.

35. See www.ausable.org/or.fora.cfm

Chapter 6: Individuals can *make a difference*
1. Yvonne Roberts, *The Observer*, Sunday 15 December 2002, commenting on: 'Banishing Scrooge, the Cost of Christmas'. A report conducted by The Family Welfare Association.

2. For an authoritative guide to decreasing personal carbon emissions, see Goodall, C. (2007) *How to Live a Low-carbon Life. The Individual's Guide to Stopping Climate Change,* London: Earthscan.

3. Goodall (2007) pp. 73–75.

4. See www.sageoxford.org.uk/ecohouse.htm There will be more about Sage in the next chapter.

5. For a detailed discussion on cars, see Goodall (2007) pp. 175–209.

6. Goodall (2007) pp. 217–228.

7. See details of the LOAF Campaign on the CEL website: www.christian-ecology.org.uk/loaf.htm

8. Hickman, L. (2005) *A Good Life. The Guide to Ethical Living,* London: Guardian Books, pp. 19ff.

9. Browne, A. and Yeoman, F. (2007) Food patriotism and the political battle over your shopping basket. *The Times,* 4 January 2007, p 6.

10. Anon (2006) Voting with your trolley. *The Economist,* 9 December 2006, pp. 81–83.

11. Hickman (2005), pp. 26–28.

12. See www.food.gov.uk/

13. The Soil Association website: www.soilassociation.org/

14. For the connection between Peak Oil and food production, see Porritt, J. (2007) Banana drama. Declining oil reserves will impact hugely on energy prices and the way we eat and farm. Is Britain ready for a new agri-culture? The Guardian, Wednesday 24 January

2007. Also available at
http://environment.guardian.co.uk/food/story/0,,1997432,00.html

15. The Asian Rural Institute: www.ari-edu.org/english/index.html

16. Anon (2006) Good Food? *The Economist*, 9 December 2006, p. 11.

17. See section 23 (e) at
www.fco.gov.uk/Files/kfile/PostG8_Gleneagles_Africa,0.pdf

18. See: www.earthresources.org.uk/index.php

19. See: www.freecycle.org/

20. See www.svenskakyrkan.se/vaxjostift Växjö diocese in Sweden and Oxford Diocese twinned in 2003. The bags have their web address on them.

21. Gardner, G., Assadourian, E. and Sarin R. (2004) The state of consumption today. In State of the World 2004. A Worldwatch Institute report on progress toward a sustainable society. New York: W.W. Norton & Company, pp. 3–21. Also available in PDF format from www.worldwatch.org/

22. See: Smith, D. (2007) Stop shopping ... or the planet will go pop. *The Observer*, Sunday 8 April 2007. Also available at
http://observer.guardian.co.uk/uk_news/story/0,,2052490,00.html

23. For a very practical way to downsize your lifestyle, see Living Lightly 24:1 (www.livinglightly24-1.org.uk), a simpler, greener lifestyle commitment from A Rocha, based on the radical idea that 'the earth is the Lord's and all that is in it' (Psalm 24:1).

Chapter 7: Caring as communities

1. This was said at the Faithworks awards ceremony 2006. For further information about Faithworks, see www.faithworks.info

2. Walsh, J.R. and Bradley, T. (1991) *A History of the Irish Church, 400–700 AD*, Dublin: The Columba Press, pp. 160–163.

3. Hodson, M.R. (2000) *A Feast of Seasons*, London: Monarch

4. See, for example, 1 and 2 Timothy and Titus.

5. See Hauerwas, S (1981) *A Community of Character. Toward a Constructive Christian Social Ethic*, Notre Dame: Notre Dame Press; and Fergusson, D. (1998) *Community, Liberalism and Christian Ethics*, Cambridge: CUP.

6. Farnell, R. (2001) Faith communities, regeneration and social exclusion: developing a research agenda. *Community Development Journal* **36**, 263–272.

7. See www.faithworks.info

8. For further information on eco-housing, see www.sustainable-build.co.uk/EcoHousingUK.html

9. In March 1963, Dr Richard Beeching published a report 'The Re-Shaping of British Railways'. It proposed the closing of almost one-third of British railway lines and 2,000 stations.

10. Cornerstone Christian Centre, 10 Savile Way, Grove, Wantage, Oxon., OX12 0PT. Tel: 01235 772280.

11. See www.transitiontowns.org

12. See www.wwf.org.uk

13. See www.sd-commission.org.uk

14. WWF-UK and the Sustainable Development Commission (2005) Sustainable development and UK faith groups. Two sides of the same coin? London: WWF-UK and SDC. Also available at www.sd-commission.org.uk/pages/faith.html

15. See www.stsidwells.org.uk

16. See www.sageoxford.org.uk

17. See www.webarchive.org.uk

18. See Chapter 10 for the story of this association.

19. See www.ouwg.org.uk

20. See www.freshexpressions.org.uk

21. See www.ssmjchurchyard.org.uk

22. See www.ecocongregation.org

23. This article was originally published in *Sage Words* (January 2006)

Chapter 8: National leadership will inspire change

1. This quote, thought to be from Plato, can be found at the entrance to the Department of Justice Building, Washington, D.C.

2. Job 42:1–6.

3. This reflection is based on some of the principles outlined in: Smith, C. & Elmes, M. (2002) Leading change: Insights from Jungian interpretations of the book of Job. *Journal of Organizational Change Management* **15**, 448–460.

4. Bovine spongiform encephalopathy, also known as mad cow disease.

5. See http://news.bbc.co.uk/1/hi/uk/6917253.stm

6. Tulip, K. and Michaels, L. (2004) *A Rough Guide to the UK Farming Crisis*, Oxford: Corporate Watch.

7. John is also the Chair of the Steering Group for the Certificate in Christian Rural and Environmental Studies (CRES), for which Martin Hodson is Principal Tutor. See www.cres.org.uk

8. MAFF, the UK government's Ministry of Agriculture, Fisheries and Food. Most of its functions were transferred to the Department for Environment, Food and Rural Affairs (DEFRA) in 2001, with food going to the Food Standards Agency (FSA).

9. For more details, see www.fcn.org.uk

10. Royal Agricultural Benevolent Institution. See www.rabi.org.uk/index.html

11. See www.arc-addingtonfund.org.uk/index.htm

12. The helpline number is 07002 326 326.

13. It might be possible to use carbon recapture systems in the future, but these are still in development, and will require considerable energy to run.

14. See www.defra.gov.uk/news/latest/2007/climate-0313.htm

15. See www.stopclimatechaos.org

16. Department of Trade and Industry (2007) *Meeting the Energy Challenge*, A White Paper on Energy. TSO: Norwich.

17. See www.westmill.coop

18. For more details on biomass, see www.biomassenergycentre.org.uk

19. Spencer, N. and White, R. (2007) *Christianity, Climate Change and Sustainable Living*, SPCK: London, p. 193.

20. DEFRA (2007) UK Biomass Strategy. London: DEFRA.

21. Department of Trade and Industry (2007) A White Paper on Energy, p. 195.

22. See www.eci.ox.ac.uk

23. These are also known as DTQs (Domestic Tradable Quotas).

24. DEFRA is the UK government's Department for Environment, Food and Rural Affairs. See www.defra.gov.uk

25. Spencer and White (2007), p. 186.

26. Goodall, C. (2007) *How to Live a Low-carbon Life. The Individual's Guide to Stopping Climate Change*, London: Earthscan, p. 41.

27. For more detailed accounts of the advantages and disadvantages of PCAs and carbon taxation, see Spencer and White (2007), pp. 177–186; and Goodall (2007), pp. 39–41.

28. A good source for material on the controversy over the London congestion charge is http://en.wikipedia.org/wiki/London_congestion_charge#Traffic_levels

29. See www.simoncollings.co.uk

30. Rogers, E.M. (1962) *Diffusion of Innovations*, New York: Free Press of Glencoe.

31. http://en.wikipedia.org/wiki/Diffusion_of_innovations

32. See www.methodist.org.uk/index.cfm?fuseaction=opentogod.content&cmid=350

33. See www.urc.org.uk/our_work/committees/church_society/environment_policy.htm

34. See www.catholicchurch.org.uk/resource/GreenText/index.htm

35. Foster, C. (2005) *Sharing God's Planet: A Christian Vision for a Sustainable Future,* Church House Publishing: London. Also available at www.cofe.anglican.org/about/gensynod/agendas/gs1558.pdf

36. See www.shrinkingthefootprint.cofe.anglican.org

37. Foster, C. and Shreeve, D. (2007) *How Many Lightbulbs Does It Take to Change a Christian? Pocket Guide to Shrinking your Ecological Footprint,* London: Church House Publishing; and Straine, G. and Oxley, N. (2007) *For Creed and Creation. A Simple Guidebook for Running a Greener Church,* Aldgate Press: London. Also available from www.shrinkingthefootprint.cofe.anglican.org/stf_creedcreation_mar07.pdf

38. See www.eenonline.org

39. See www.christian-ecology.org.uk

40. See www.operationnoah.org

41. See http://creationcare.org

42. For a detailed analysis of the Declaration, see Berry, R.J. (ed.) (2000) *The Care of Creation. Focusing Concern and Action,* Leicester: IVP.

43. Barry, D. and Elmes, M. (1997) Strategy retold: Toward a narrative view of strategic discourse. *The Academy of Management Review* **22**, 429–452.

Chapter 9: Uniting with the Global South

1. Delivered by Kennedy before a joint session of the US Congress (25 May 1961).

2. See www.allnations.ac.uk

3. This project is being supported as a carbon offset scheme sponsored by the Wakefield Diocese in the UK: www.wakefield.anglican.org/info/overseas/mara/maratrees.htm

4. The Bishop was writing in August 2007, and referring to the exceptional rainfall and floods in the UK that year.

5. Sacks, J. (1995) Faith for the Future. London: Darton, Longman and Todd.

6. See Steger, M.B. (2003) *Globalization. A Very Short Introduction*, Oxford: OUP, p. 13.

7. Potter, R.B., Binns, T., Elliott, J.A. and Smith, D. (2004) *Geographies of Development*, 2nd edn, Harlow: Pearson Education Ltd, p. 131.

8. See Chapter 4.

9. Sider, R.J. (1977) *Rich Christians in an age of hunger*, Sevenoaks: Hodder and Stoughton.

10. Sider (1977), p. 12.

11. Leibowitz, N. (1980) *New Studies in Vayikra, Leviticus*, Jerusalem: WZO, Dept. for Torah Education and Culture in the Diaspora.

12. Sider (1977), p. 79.

13. See Chapter 1.

14. See the Jubilee Debt Campaign website: www.jubileedebtcampaign.org.uk/

15. Potter et al. (2004), p. 355.

16. Kessler, J.J. and Van Dorp, M. (1998) Structural adjustment and the environment: The need for an analytical methodology. *Ecological Economics* **27**, 267–281.

17. Potter et al. (2004), p. 35.

18. This figure was calculated by an economist at the World Bank. See: Elliot, L. (2002) A cure worse than the disease. *The Guardian*, Monday 21 January.

19. See Chapter 4 for a discussion of human population issues.

20. Meadows, D.H., Meadows, D.L., Randers, J. and Behrens, W.W. (1972) *The Limits to Growth*, New York: Universe Books.

21. The Report of the Brundtland Commission, *Our Common Future*, was published by Oxford University Press in 1987. The full

text can be downloaded as a scanned copy of the UN General Assembly document A/42/427 at http://ringofpeace.org/environment/brundtland.html

22. Berry, R.J. (ed.) (2007) *When Enough is Enough*, Leicester: Apollos, IVP, pp. 18–20.

23. Spencer, N. and White, R. (2007) *Christianity, Climate Change and Sustainable Living*, London: SPCK, pp. 35–38.

24. We had this report from Lesley Bilinda, a widow of the Rwanda massacre who had been in the country in October 2006, where she saw young crops dead in the fields for lack of rain.

25. Patz, J.A., Campbell-Lendrum, D., Holloway, T. and Foley, J.A. (2005) Impact of regional climate change on human health. *Nature,* **438**, 310–317.

26. Myers, N. (2002) Environmental refugees: A growing phenomenon of the 21st century. *Philosophical Transactions of the Royal Society of London, Series B* **357**, 609–613.

27. Weaver, J. and Hodson, M.R. (2007) *The Place of Environmental Theology: A Guide for Seminaries, Colleges and Universities*, Oxford: Whitley Trust and Prague: IBTS, p. 67.

28. Christian Aid report (2006) *The Climate of Poverty: Facts, Fears and Hope*, London: Christian Aid.

29. See www.cms-uk.org

30. See Chapter 1.

31. Lord May, the former Chief Scientific Adviser to the UK government, gave this figure in a lecture at Jesus College, Oxford on 8 February 2007.

32. See www.ari-edu.org/english/index.html

33. Uphoff's group have a website on SRI at http://ciifad.cornell.edu/sri/

34. Surridge, C. (2004) Feast or famine? *Nature* **428**, 360–361.

35. McDonald, A.J., Hobbs P.R. and Riha, S.J. (2006) Does the system of rice intensification outperform conventional best

management? A synopsis of the empirical record. *Field Crops Research* **96**, 31–36.

36. See www.gci.org.uk/contconv/cc.html

37. See Spencer, N. and White, R. (2007), pp. 208–213.

Chapter 10: Dreams and visions
1. From the conclusion to an address given at the Anniversary Meeting of the Royal Society on 30 November 2006. See www.royalsoc.ac.uk/publication.asp?id=5664

2. See Chapter 7 for the origins and work of Sage.

3. A Rocha means "The Rock" in Portuguese. It is now an international organization with work in many countries. See http://en.arocha.org for details.

4. Will Simonson is now Scientific Director for A Rocha.

5. Perhaps we should mention here that Martin and Margot first met in October 1993, and were married in April 1996. Sage took part in the wedding ceremony.

6. See: Harris, P. (1993) *Under the Bright Wings*, London: Hodder and Stoughton: the story of the first ten years of A Rocha. For some time it was out of print, but was reprinted in 2000 in Canada by Regent Publishing, in paperback, with a brief update added. *Kingfisher's Fire* (a kind of sequel to *Under the Bright Wings*) is now with the publishers (Monarch) and scheduled to appear in January 2008.

7. The work in Portugal has continued, now under A Rocha Portugal. See http://en.arocha.org/portugal

8. See Chapter 8 for John Neal's story.

9. See the Chiltern Gateway project at www.chilterngateway.org.uk

10. See www.sageoxford.org.uk/envsun2007.htm

11. Humphrys, J. (2001) *The Great Food Gamble*, London: Hodder and Stoughton, pp. 195–227.

12. Yonekura-Sakakibara, K. and Saito, K. (2006) Review: Genetically modified plants for the promotion of human health.

Biotechnology Letters **28**, 1983–1991.

13. Bruce, D. and Horrocks, D. (eds) (2001) *Modifying Creation? GM Crops and Foods: A Christian Perspective*, Carlisle: Paternoster Press.

14. Bryant, J.A., Baggott la Velle, L. and Searle, J. (2005) *Introduction to Bioethics*, Chichester: Wiley, p. 96.

15. Andow, D.A. and Zwahlen, C. (2006) Assessing environmental risks of transgenic plants. *Ecology Letters* **9**, 196–214.

16. Bruce and Horrocks (2001), p. 118.

17. See www.gmnation.co.uk for the results.

18. For a report on the Dorchester Abbey debate by Canon Christopher Hall, see www.sageoxford.org.uk/dorabbgm.htm

19. From the executive summary of the GM debate at www.gmnation.co.uk/ut_09/ut_9_6.htm#summary

20. See the Friends of the Earth website at www.foe.co.uk/campaigns/real_food/press_for_change/email_la/index.shtml

21. A version of this story was first published in the Ecocolumn in *The Door*, Oxford's Diocesan Newspaper, September 2007.

22. Davies, E.W. (1999) Walking in God's ways: The concept of imitatio Dei in the Old Testament. in E. Ball (ed.) *In Search of True Wisdom: Essays in Old Testament Interpretation in Honour of Ronald E. Clements*, Sheffield: Sheffield Academic Press, pp. 99–115.

23. For a more detailed summary of this material, see Houghton, J. (2007) The challenge of sustainability. In R.J. Berry (ed.) *When Enough is Enough. A Christian Framework for Environmental Sustainability*, Nottingham: Apollos IVP, pp. 50–68.

24. See www.ipcc.ch

25. The full statement is at www.ucsusa.org/ucs/about/1992-world-scientists-warning-to-humanity.html

26. The Stern Review on the Economics of Climate Change can be accessed at:
www.hm-treasury.gov.uk/independent_reviews/stern_review_economics_climate_change/sternreview_index.cfm

27. Craston, C. (ed.) (1994) *By Word and Deed*, London: Church House Publishing, p. 57.

28. Berry, R.J. (ed.) (2000) *The Care of Creation. Focusing Concern and Action*, Leicester: IVP, p. 15.

29. The full version of the Declaration can be found in Berry, R.J. (ed.) (2000) pp. 17–22.

30. Berry (2000).

31. For a commentary on these, see Mission Theological Advisory Group (2002) *Presence and Prophecy: A Heart for Mission in Theological Education*, London: Church House Publishing, pp. 30–34.

32. Craston (1994), p.46

33. Craston (1994), p. 33

34. See www.anglicancommunion.org/ethics_technology/introducing_the_network.cfm

35. Sadly, the website for Climate Forum 2002 was taken down in the summer of 2007

36. See www.jri.org.uk

37. See www.ausable.org

38. See Little, A.G. (2005) Cizik Matters: An interview with green evangelical leader Richard Cizik: www.grist.org/news/maindish/2005/10/05/cizik

39. See www.nae.net

40. To view the Sandy Cove Covenant, go to www.creationcare.org/conference

41. See www.nae.net/images/civic_responsibility2.pdf

42. This was seen as so significant that it was reported in both *Science* and *Nature*, the two top scientific journals in the world: Kintisch, E. (2006) Evangelicals, scientists reach common ground on climate change. *Science* **311**, 1082–1083; and Haag, A. (2006) Church joins crusade over climate change. *Nature* **440**, 136–137.

43. A recording of the service is available at
www.jesus.ox.ac.uk/chapel/sundayworship.php

Chapter 11: Hope and the resurrection of creation

1. For more detail, see the end of Chapter 4, where we have put a summary of the problems.

2. Houghton, J.T. (2007) The challenge of sustainability. In R.J. Berry (ed.) *When Enough is Enough: A Christian Framework for Environmental Sustainability*, Leicester: Apollos, IVP, p. 62. See also www.jesus.ox.ac.uk/chapel/sundayworship.php

3. Wright, N.T. (2003) *The Resurrection of the Son of God*, London: SPCK, p. 239.

4. See www.stonechurch.ca

5. Orr, D.W. (2005) Armageddon versus extinction. *Conservation Biology* **19**, 290–292.

6. Stuart, S.N. et al. (2005) Conservation theology for conservation biologists – a reply to David Orr. *Conservation Biology* **19**, 1689–1692. This article has 30 authors, including many of the most well-known Christian environmentalists.

7. Wright, N.T. (2006) *New Heavens, New Earth. The Biblical Picture of Christian Hope*, 2nd edn. Grove Books: Cambridge.

8. Press, W.H. (2000) It won't come to the crunch. *Nature* **405**, 395–396 (25 May). This is a review of Goldsmith, D.W. (2000) *The Runaway Universe: The Race to Find the Future of the Cosmos*, New York: Perseus Books.

9. Bauckham, R. (1993) *The Theology of Revelation*, Cambridge: CUP, pp. 48–53.

10. Bauckham (1993), p. 53.

11. The hymn "The story of Jesus" was written by Maria Matilda Penstone (1859–1910) with music by C.B. Jutson (1870–1930). It is available as hymn 857 in *The Methodist Hymn Book* (1933) London: The Methodist Church, p. 753.

12. Eurostar moved their London terminus to St Pancras in November 2007.

13. See www.eurostar.com

14. Eurostar has announced plans in 2007 to decrease its carbon footprint even further. Part of the reason for its low carbon emissions is that is runs on French electricity, which is generated with nuclear power.

15. See www.br.fgov.be

16. See www.htbrussels.com

17. See Chapter 6 for more on Eco-Congregation.

18. At Holy Trinity, Brussels we met Denzil Walton, who has written a series of guides to walks in the area. The one we used was Walton, D. (2006) *Tervuren. Nature Walks near Brussels*, Kortenberg, Belgium: Linx Publications.

19. See www.africamuseum.be

Useful Websites

A Rocha, Christians in Conservation, is an international organisation with centres in an ever increasing number of countries (See Chapter 10). *www.arocha.org*

Anglican Communion Environmental Network (ACEN) aims to encourage Anglicans to support sustainable environmental practices as individuals and in the life of their communities (See Chapter 10).
www.anglicancommunion.org/ethics_technology/introducing_the_network.cfm

The Asian Rural Institute (ARI) in Japan is a Christian foundation that trains development workers and pastors in sustainable agriculture (See Chapters 6 and 9).
www.ari-edu.org/english/index.html

Au Sable Institute of Environmental Studies was founded in 1980 in the United States. It runs courses and conferences bringing together scientists and theologians to further the Christian understanding of the environment (See Chapter 10).
www.ausable.org

Christian Aid is an agency of the churches in the UK and Ireland that strives for a new world transformed by an end to poverty (See Chapter 9).
www.christianaid.org.uk

Christian Ecology Link is a multi-denominational UK Christian organisation for people concerned about the environment (See Chapter 8).
www.christian-ecology.org.uk

Christian Rural Concern (CRuC) aims to spread a Christian understanding of rural and environmental issues in the UK.
www.cruc.org.uk

Christian Rural and Environmental Studies (CRES) runs certificate and diploma courses by distance learning. CRES is jointly run by Christian Rural Concern and the John Ray Initiative, and is validated by Ripon College Cuddesdon, nr. Oxford, UK. Martin Hodson is Principal Tutor for CRES.
www.cres.org.uk

Eco-congregation encourages churches in the UK to consider environmental issues within a Christian context (See Chapter 7).
www.ecocongregation.org

European Christian Environmental Network has links to many Christian environmental groups and resources across Europe.
www.ecen.org

Evangelical Environmental Network (EEN) from North America is a non-profit organization that seeks to educate, inspire, and mobilize Christians in their effort to care for God's creation (See Chapter 8).
www.creationcare.org

Farm Crisis Network (FCN) aims to relieve need, hardship and distress in the farming community in the UK by providing pastoral and practical support (See Chapter 8). *www.farmcrisisnetwork.org.uk*

The John Ray Initiative (JRI) aims to bring together Christian and scientific understanding of the environment. Martin and Margot Hodson have been very involved with JRI since the Climate Forum 2002 meeting (See Chapter 10). *www.jri.org.uk*

Milton Keynes Christian Environmental Group is a new (2007) group operating in Milton Keynes, UK. It has a passion to help promote, highlight and challenge environmental issues within Christian churches and organisations in Milton Keynes. *http://mkchristianenvironment.wordpress.com*

Nueva Creacion is a Christian Institute for Ecology and Development based in Lima, Peru (they have an English version of their website). *www.nuevacreacion.info/ingles/home.html*

Operation Noah is the UK churches' climate change campaign. *www.operationnoah.org*

Plateau Perspectives is a non-profit organization that supports local initiatives in conservation and sustainable development in the Tibetan Plateau region of China. *www.plateauperspectives.org*

Sage, Oxford's Christian Environmental Group was founded in 1990 in Oxford, UK. Martin Hodson was one of the founding members and runs their website (See Chapters 7 and 10).

www.sageoxford.org.uk

Tearfund is an international Christian development agency working with the world's poor (See Chapter 9).

www.tearfund.org

Jesus College Climate Change Service. A BBC Radio broadcast of a service from Jesus College, Oxford, UK on 11 February 2007. The service was led by Margot Hodson and the preacher was Sir John Houghton (See Foreword and Chapter 10).

www.jesus.ox.ac.uk/chapel/sundayworship.php

Index

Biblical Index

Certificate in Christian Rural and Environmental Studies

This is a course that is ideal for all who are concerned for the environment. It will also be of interest to anyone in rural ministry, whether ordained or lay. The course is run by Christian Rural Concern and The John Ray Initiative, and is based at Ripon College Cuddesdon, near Oxford. It offers an opportunity for integrated study:

- Part time modular course by distance learning
- A local personal tutor
- Flexibility to tailor coursework topics to your own particular concerns
- Opportunities to meet with other participants
- Core modules which approach rural and environmental studies from a Christian viewpoint
- Additional modules giving the opportunity to specialise in either rural or environmental concerns
- Certificate accredited by Ripon College Cuddesdon
- Usually taken over two years
- Current cost (2008) is £690 in total, which includes two residential weekends, payable in two annual instalments

Principal Tutor: Dr Martin J. Hodson

Full details from:
Mrs Dena Burne,
01242 528321
secretary@cres.org.uk
www.cres.org.uk